The Southwest

Titles in the series:

The Northeast
The Southeast
The Midwest
The West
The Southwest

The Southwest

GREENWOOD PRESS
Westport, Connecticut • London

Library of Congress Cataloging-in-Publication Data

Creative Media Applications
  How geography affects the United States/Creative Media Applications.
  p. cm.
  Summary: Explores the ways in which geography has affected the lives of the people of the United States.
  Includes bibliographical references (p.).
  Contents: v.1. Northeast — v.2. Southeast — v.3. Midwest — v.4. West — v.5. Southwest.
  ISBN 0-313-32250-3 (set) — 0-313-32251-1 (Northeast) — 0-313-32252-X (Southeast) — 0-313-32253-8 (Midwest) — 0-313-32254-6 (West) — 0-313-32255-4 (Southwest)
  1. United States — Geography — Juvenile literature. 2. Human geography — United States — Juvenile literature. 3. United States — History, Local — Juvenile literature. 4. Regionalism — United States — Juvenile literature. [1. United States — Geography.] I. Creative Media Applications.

E161.3.H69 2002
304.2'0973—dc21   2002075304

British Library Cataloguing in Publication Data is available.

Library of Congress Catalog Card Number: 2002075304
ISBN: 0-313-32250-3   (set)
        0-313-32251-1   (Northeast)
        0-313-32252-X   (Southeast)
        0-313-32253-8   (Midwest)
        0-313-32254-6   (West)
        0-313-32255-4   (Southwest)

First published in 2002

Greenwood Press, 88 Post Road West, Westport, CT 06881
An imprint of Greenwood Publishing Group, Inc.
www.greenwood.com

Printed in the United States of America

♾™

The paper used in this book complies with the Permanent Paper Standard issued by the National Information Standards Organization (Z39.48–1984).

10   9   8   7   6   5   4   3   2   1

A Creative Media Applications, Inc. Production
Writer: Robin Doak
Design and Production: Fabia Wargin Design, Inc.
Editor: Matt Levine
Copyeditor: Laurie Lieb
Proofreader: Tania Bissell
AP Photo Researcher: Yvette Reyes
Consultant: Dean M. Hanink, Department of Geography,
      University of Connecticut
Maps: Ortelius Design

Photo Credits:
Cover: ©Photodisc, Inc.
©Photodisc, Inc., *pages:* ix, xi
AP/Wide World Photographs *pages:* 4, 6, 11, 12, 13, 14, 17, 22, 32, 36, 39, 41, 49, 54, 56, 58, 66, 74, 77, 82, 90, 95, 97, 103, 108, 115, 116, 121, 125
©CORBIS *page:* 28
©Bettmann/CORBIS *pages:* 27, 31, 47, 50, 65, 84
©Medford Historical Society Collection/CORBIS *pages:* 65, 105, 106
©Craig Aurness/CORBIS *page:* 87
©Museum of the City of New York/CORBIS *page:* 89

Contents

Introduction vii

Chapter **1** Colorado River 1

Chapter **2** Great Plains 19

Chapter **3** Gulf of Mexico 43

Chapter **4** Red River 61

Chapter **5** Rio Grande...79

Chapter **6** Rocky Mountains............................99

Chapter **7** Sonoran Desert 111

Sources 127

Index..128

Introduction

The Southwest region of the United States is bordered by the Southeast region to the east, Mexico and the Gulf of Mexico to the south, the West region to the west, and the West and Midwest regions to the north. There are four states in the Southwest: Arizona, New Mexico, Oklahoma, and Texas.

The Southwest has a variety of landforms, from hot, dry deserts to grassy rolling plains to sandy beaches along the Gulf of Mexico. The area's wealth of natural resources has made the area important in our nation's history and economy. Some of the earliest European exploration occurred in the Southwest. Beginning in the 1700s, different groups, including Native Americans, Spanish, Mexicans, and Americans, fought for control of the region.

The climate of the Southwest tends to be warmer and drier than other parts of the nation. Long, hot summers; low humidity; and mild winters have attracted residents and visitors alike to the area.

Between 1990 and 2000, the Southwest was one of the fastest-growing regions in the nation. Arizona's population increased by 40 percent during that period. It was second in growth only to Nevada. In addition, four of the ten most populated cities in the United States are located in the Southwest: Houston (HYOO-stin), Texas (fourth); Phoenix (FEE-nix), Arizona (sixth); Dallas, Texas (eighth); and San Antonio, Texas (tenth).

A Unique Heritage

The earliest people to settle in the Southwest may have arrived more than 11,000 years ago. These early people included the Clovis and Folsom cultures. They fashioned spear points out of rocks and hunted mammoths (large creatures related to elephants), bison, and other big animals.

Later groups included the Anasazi (an-uh-SAH-zee), who hunted and farmed in the Southwest. The Anasazi are known for their magnificent, multistoried cliff dwellings. When the first Europeans began exploring the Southwest, tribes in the region included the Caddo, Comanche (kuh-MAN-chee), Kiowa (KYE-oh-wuh), Pueblo (PWEB-loh), Tohono O'odham (toh-HOH-noh AH-ah-tum), and Yuma (YOO-muh).

For nearly 300 years, the Spanish controlled the Southwest. The first Spanish expedition into the region was conducted by Francisco Vásquez de Coronado (fran-SISS-koh VAHS-kez deh kor-oh-NAH-doh) in 1540. After Coronado's expedition, Spanish settlers trickled into the Southwest from New Spain (Mexico), establishing missions, forts, and settlements. In 1821, Mexico won its independence (in-duh-PEN-dense) from Spain, and the Southwest became a Mexican territory. However, Mexico lost control of the region after being defeated by the United States in the Mexican War (1846–1848).

Perhaps more than any other region in the United States, the Southwest still retains echoes of its rich past. Numerous Native American reservations are located throughout the region, especially (es-PESH-ul-ee) in Oklahoma. As a result of three centuries of Spanish influence (IN-floo-ense), the Southwest region also has a distinct Spanish flavor.

This adobe house in Santa Fe, New Mexico is an example of Spanish architecture that can be found throughout the Southwest.

With its warm, sunny climate and unique (yoo-NEEK) blend of cultures, the Southwest continues to attract people from around the world. The region is important to the nation's economy, as well. Oil and natural gas are two important Southwestern products. Farmlands and ranches in the area are major sources of food for the United States.

STATE BIRTHDAYS

Some of the Southwestern states were among the first to be explored, yet the last to be accepted as part of the United States.

State	Capital	First Permanent Settlement	Date of Statehood	Order of Statehood
Arizona	Phoenix	Tubac, 1752	February 14, 1912	48
New Mexico	Santa Fe	San Gabriel, 1598	January 6, 1912	47
Oklahoma	Oklahoma City	Salina, 1817	November 16, 1907	46
Texas	Austin	Ysleta, 1680	December 29, 1845	28

MORE STATE STATS

The largest state in the Southwest is Texas, with nearly 262,000 square miles (681,200 square kilometers) of land. The smallest Southwestern state is Oklahoma. Here, the Southwestern states are ordered from smallest to largest.

State	Size (land and water)	Size Rank	Population	State Rank
Oklahoma	68,679 square miles (178,565 sq. kilometers)	19	3,450,654	27
Arizona	113,642 square miles (295,469 sq. kilometers)	6	5,130,632	20
New Mexico	121,364 square miles (315,546 sq. kilometers)	5	1,819,046	36
Texas	261,914 square miles (680,976 sq. kilometers)	2	20,851,820	2

NOTE: All metric conversions in this book are approximate.

The sandstone cliffs of Antelope Canyon near Page, Arizona have eroded into unusual shapes that inspire photographers from throughout the world.

Colorado River

1

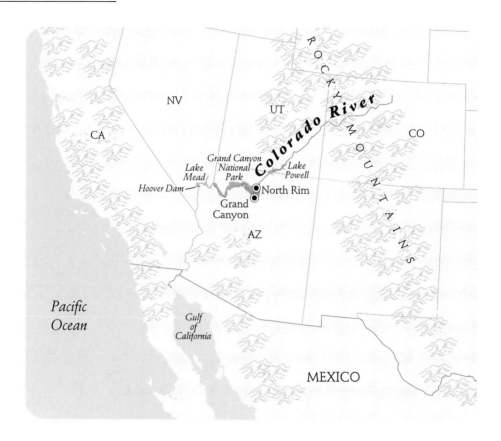

One of the major rivers of the Southwest, the Colorado River, flows for 1,450 miles (2,320 kilometers) from its source in the Rocky Mountains of Colorado. As it winds its way to the Pacific (puh-SIFF-ik) Ocean, the Colorado passes through five states: Colorado, Utah, Arizona, Nevada, and California. It flows through northwest Mexico and into the Gulf of California. Along the way, the Colorado receives the waters of several *tributaries* (smaller rivers and streams), including the Little Colorado and Gila Rivers. It drains about 250,000 square miles (650,000 square kilometers) of land in seven states.

The river has etched a distinct pathway through the Southwest. Over millions of years, the Colorado carved a trail deep into the earth. It formed towering cliffs and deep canyons in the rocky soil. More than

1,000 miles (1,600 kilometers) of the river flow through cliffs and canyons.

In northwestern Arizona, the Colorado has created the most famous canyon in the world: the Grand Canyon. The Grand Canyon is nearly 1 mile deep (1.6 kilometers) and up to 16 miles (25.6 kilometers) wide in some spots. The Colorado River runs for 217 miles (347 kilometers) through this big hole in the ground.

• Fast Fact •

The Colorado River forms most of Arizona's western boundary, separating the state from Nevada and California.

The Colorado is an important source of water for surrounding areas. Parts of the river have been dammed to provide water for cities and towns in California, Nevada, and other states. The river area itself, however, is sparsely populated, with few cities located along its banks.

Settlement

Some of the earliest people to visit the Colorado River and Grand Canyon were hunters who arrived in the region as early as 10,000 years ago. These early people did not settle near the Colorado. They were just passing through, probably following the animals that they hunted. The first arrivals did, however, leave traces behind. They hid figures of animals, made out of willow twigs, inside the cliffside caves.

• Fast Fact •

Spanish explorers named the river *Rio Colorado,* **or "red river," for its reddish-brown waters.**

Chaco Canyon, New Mexico is the home of Anasazi ruins that are approximately 1,000 years old.

One of the first peoples to settle in the area was the Anasazi (an-uh-SAH-zee) people. The Anasazi, ancestors (AN-sess-terz) of the Pueblo (PWEB-loh) people, lived along the river around A.D. 100. Some later moved into the cliffs. There, they constructed large, multistory dwellings out of masonry and adobe (uh-DOH-bee), which is sun-baked clay. Around 1300, the Anasazi left the Colorado River area, possibly to escape a drought (DROWT) and find fertile land for farming.

• Fast Fact •

The name *Anasazi* (an-uh-SAH-zee) comes from a Navajo (NAV-uh-hoh) word that means "ancient ones."

Today, hundreds of Anasazi and Pueblo ruins dot the canyons and riverside. One dwelling, called Pueblo Bonito, had more than 800 rooms and was five stories in height. At Grand Canyon National Park, visitors can see Anasazi storehouses in the canyon walls. They can also visit Tusayan Pueblo, a U-shaped village built in the late 1100s.

Later tribes who settled along the river included the Pueblo people—Zuñi (ZOON-yee) and Hopi (HOH-pee)—Paiute (PYE-yoot), Ute (YOOT), and Yuma (YOO-muh). The Navajo (NAV-uh-hoh) people arrived in the region around 1600. Another area tribe was the Havasupai (hah-vuh-SOO-pye), the only tribe that still lives in the canyons today.

Today, the Colorado River Indian Tribes (CRIT) live on a reservation that spans the river from La Paz County, Arizona, to San Bernardino County, California. The reservation was set up in 1865 as a home for tribes who lived along the river. Today, the CRIT include the members of the Mohave (moh-HAHV-ee), Chemehuevi (chem-uh-WHAY-vee), Hopi, and Navajo tribes.

The first Europeans to see the Colorado River and Grand Canyon were the Spanish. In 1540, Francisco Vásquez de Coronado (fran-SISS-koh VAHS-kez deh kor-oh-NAH-doh) set out from New Spain (Mexico) to search for the Seven Cities of Gold. These fabled cities were said to exist in what is today the Southwestern United States. During the journey, Coronado sent Garcia Lopez de Cardeñas (car-DAYN-yahss) to explore the Colorado River. Cardeñas hoped to follow the river to the Pacific Ocean, where supply ships were waiting.

Although Cardeñas did not reach the waiting ships, he became the first nonnative person to see the Grand Canyon. The captain ordered some of his men to climb down the canyon's wall, but this proved impossible. After trying for three days to reach the river below, he and his men gave up and headed back to Coronado.

At the end of the river, Hernando de Alarcón (ahl-ar-KOHN) was waiting with the supply ships. Alarcón was the first nonnative to explore the lower river. He managed to travel about 100 miles (160 kilometers) upstream before turning back. He waited for several weeks for Coronado to appear and then returned to New Spain.

The Grand Canyon stretches into the distance in this photograph taken from the Widforss Trail on the canyon's north rim.

NORTH RIM, SOUTH RIM

The Grand Canyon has two rims, or edges: the North Rim and the South Rim. The North Rim, on the north side of the canyon, is heavily forested. It is up to 1,000 feet (300 meters) higher than the South Rim in spots. The South Rim is more than 200 miles (320 kilometers) away by road from the North Rim, on the south side of the canyon. The North Rim is more difficult to reach from populated regions than the South Rim. Also, North Rim roads are sometimes closed in the winter when there is heavy snowfall. As a result, the South Rim receives far more visitors. In fact, nine out of ten Grand Canyon tourists visit only the South Rim.

Although the Spanish would continue their explorations of the lower river, they did not settle the Colorado River region. They considered the land mostly unusable. Because there were no cities of gold on its banks, the river was undesirable to them.

American Exploration

In the Mexican War (1846–1848), the United States and Mexico came to blows over the ownership of Texas, California, and much of the Southwest. Both nations wanted control of these important pieces of land. The war ended in February 1848, when the two nations signed the Treaty of Guadalupe Hidalgo (gwahd-uh-LOOP hih-DAHL-goh). Under the terms of the treaty, Mexico gave up 500,000 acres (200,000 hectares)—two-fifths of its territory—in exchange for $15 million.

Once the war had ended, the United States decided to survey its new territory. One of the first expeditions to survey the Colorado River region arrived in 1858. Lieutenant (loo-TEN-ant) Joseph Ives was charged with finding whether or not the river could be easily traveled upon. Ives took a steamboat, the *Explorer*, from the mouth of the river to the Black Canyon. After the steamboat crashed into a rock, the group continued the journey, exploring parts of the Grand Canyon on foot.

The man who would bring the Colorado River and Grand Canyon to public attention arrived in the region in May 1869. John Wesley Powell, a veteran of the Civil War (1861–1865), chose nine companions to make the landmark voyage. The men started out on the Green River in Wyoming. The Green is a tributary of the Colorado.

During the thirteen-week voyage, the men covered nearly 2,000 miles (3,200 kilometers). They faced wild rapids, waterfalls, and impassible points on the river. At places where they couldn't conquer the

John Wesley Powell, seen in this late 1800s photo, was lured by science and adventure to explore the Colorado River in 1869. Powell's 99-day expedition down the water-way, and his later vision of harness-ing the river to make the Great Basin green, forever changed the river and brought enduring renown to its 35-year-old conqueror.

THE MAN WHO LOVED THE GRAND CANYON

Boating down the Colorado River was not the first adventure that John Wesley Powell undertook. As a Union officer during the Civil War (1861–1865), Powell lost his right arm at the Battle of Shiloh. Powell didn't let his injury slow him down. After the war, he became a professor at an Illinois (il-ih-NOY) university. He made several trips out west, where he got the idea to boat down the Colorado. After his famous expeditions, Powell went on to head the Geographical (jee-oh-GRAF-ik-al) and Geological (jee-oh-LAHJ-ik-al) Survey of the Rocky Mountain Region. He also helped to found the United States Geological Survey (USGS) and the Smithsonian Institute's Bureau (BYOOR-oh) of Ethnology, which studies Native American culture and language. A memorial to Powell and his achievements stands on the South Rim of the Grand Canyon.

Colorado, they dragged their boats over the land. Four of Powell's companions turned back, worried that they wouldn't live to reach the river's mouth. Ironically, three of the men who went back were killed a short time later by hostile Native Americans near the Grand Canyon.

Powell's adventures on the Colorado River brought the region to national attention. Powell kept a daily journal that was published in *Scribner's* magazine. The magazine articles, along with sketches made by a traveling companion, popularized the canyon area as a place worth seeing and preserving. One journal entry read,

JAMES WHITE'S STORY

Two years before John Wesley Powell made his way through the Grand Canyon by boat, an adventurer named James White washed up on the shores of the Colorado River near Callville, Nevada. White was delirious when he was found, but he later recovered. He had a wild tale to tell. He said that he was attacked by a group of Utes (YOOTZ). He escaped by crafting a crude log raft and floating through the Grand Canyon. If White's tale was true, this would make him the first person to complete the river journey through the canyon. Over the years, debate has raged about whether or not White could have actually completed the rough journey by raft that he described.

"The waters reel and roll and boil, and we are scarcely able to determine where we can go. Now the boat is carried to the right, perhaps close to the wall; again, she is shot into the stream, and perhaps is dragged over to the other side, where, caught in a whirlpool, she spins about. . . . The next minute a great reflex wave fills the open compartment; she is water-logged, and drifts unmanageable. Breaker after breaker rolls over her and one capsizes her. The men are thrown out; but they cling to the boat and she drifts some distance alongside of us and we are able to catch her."

Powell was fascinated by the river and its canyons. He conducted a second expedition along the river in 1871. During his two trips, Powell named the Grand Canyon and many other landmarks, including Desolation Canyon, Labyrinth Canyon, and Dirty Devil River.

"ALTOGETHER VALUELESS"

Lieutenant (loo-TEN-ant) Joseph Ives, in a report about his historic trip up the Colorado River, wrote the following about the river and Grand Canyon:

> The region . . . is, of course, altogether valueless. It can be approached only from the south, and after entering it, there is nothing to do but leave. Ours has been the first, and will doubtless be the last, party of whites to visit this profitless locality. It seems intended by nature that the Colorado River, along the greater portion of its lonely and majestic way, shall be unvisited and undisturbed.

River Towns

Because of its location, the Colorado River region in the Southwest was not heavily settled. The cliffs and canyons made most adventurers think twice about staying there. In addition, the river was considered too dangerous for shipping and travel. Although steamboats did operate on the lower river for a short time, it was a hazardous voyage. Most boats stopped operating when the railroad arrived in the 1870s.

One of the earliest towns of any size to spring up along the Colorado River in the Southwest was Yuma, Arizona. Yuma was founded during the height of the California gold rush. The town became the major river crossing for gold miners entering California from the east. Today, Yuma is a resort town where thousands of people take advantage of the warm

climate and sunny days. Nearly 55,000 people live there year-round.

Other towns got their start when the U.S. government began building dams along the river. Bullhead City, Arizona, for example, was settled as the headquarters of workers constructing Davis Dam in the 1940s. Page, Arizona, was founded in 1957 as a company town for workers building Glen Canyon Dam. Today, these two towns attract visitors who swim, boat, and fish in the lakes formed by the big dams.

The Colorado River winds its way through the steep cliffs of the Grand Canyon.

Commerce

One of the first industries along the Colorado River was fur trapping and trading. American trappers began working the river and its tributaries in the early 1800s. Miners followed the trappers. Since the 1850s, gold, silver, lead, and copper have been mined in the area. In the early days, however, the river's remote location and rough terrain made the ore difficult to haul out of the area.

One of the first big businesses in the Colorado River and Grand Canyon region was tourism. Tourists have been coming to see the Grand Canyon since 1883. These early visitors arrived in the region by stagecoach and then toured the canyon on the backs of donkeys.

In 1884, the first hotel in the region was built. Although it closed only five years later, it was just the first of many. In 1895, the Grandview Hotel was constructed, followed shortly after by the Bright Angel Lodge. Tourism really picked up in 1901, after the Santa Fe Railroad made traveling to the canyon much easier.

The Grand Canyon continues to be a top tourist spot. Each year, millions of people from around the world visit this huge canyon. Visitors can still travel to the bottom of the canyon by donkey. They can also follow in the footsteps of John Wesley Powell and brave the rapids in the canyon. Other attractions along the Colorado include Anasazi ruins and the lakes created by the river's many dams.

Rafters hit white water on the Colorado River near Glenwood Springs, Colorado.

Dams and Canals

In the driest parts of the Southwest and the West, water is a valuable natural resource. Since the early 1900s, people in these regions have looked for ways to control and use Colorado River water. Since 1901, canals and dams have been built on the river to stop flooding and to supply water for farming and power. As a result, the river is one of the most dammed waterways in the world.

The giant Hoover Dam is the largest of 50 dams controlling the Colorado River.

The "Welcome to Las Vegas" sign and the many other lights of the Neon City are powered by electricity from the dams along the Colorado River.

Before the dams were built, flooding was a problem along the river. Each spring, spring rain and melting snow from the mountains would cause the river to overflow its banks. Dams ease this problem by containing floodwaters in large lakes during the rainy season. Then during the dry season, the dams are opened up, and the water is gradually released. The dam waters are used for farming and recreation.

One of the most serious floods along the Colorado occurred in 1905. The river overflowed into the Imperial Valley in California. It filled in a large *salt sink*, a depression in the earth covered with salt. The floodwaters created a new body of water called the Salton Sea. The sea, which is much saltier than the ocean, is about 35 miles (56 kilometers) by 15 miles (24 kilometers) in size.

Four years before the Salton Sea was created, the Imperial Canal was opened for business. This 80-mile (128-kilometer) canal was the first to bring Colorado River water to the Imperial Valley. In the 1940s, the All-American Canal went into operation. This canal more efficiently (ef-FISH-ent-lee) supplied the farming area with water. Once an arid desert area, today the Imperial Valley is one of the richest areas of farmland in the nation. Farmers here grow citrus fruits, lettuce, melons, cotton, and many other crops.

In 1931, the U.S. government began building a huge dam across the Colorado River. The Hoover Dam spanned the Black Canyon between Arizona and Nevada. When completed in 1936, the dam was the largest in the world. It towered more than 720 feet (216 meters) in height and measured more than 1,240 feet (372 meters) in length.

Other dams along the Colorado include the Glen Canyon, Davis, Imperial, and Parker Dams. The dams provide water and power to cities throughout the Southwest and West. One big city that uses Colorado River electricity (ee-lek-TRISS-it-ee) is Las Vegas. In years past, the river's power helped the Neon City grow into the entertainment center that it is today.

Lakes formed by the dams provide recreation areas for people living in this dry region. Lake Mead and Lake Powell, formed by the Hoover and Glen Canyon Dams, are among the largest artificial (ar-tih-FISH-ul) lakes in the world. Thousands of people visit the lakes each year to fish, boat, water-ski, and swim.

Environmentalists point out that the dams and reservoirs (REH-zerv-wahrz) have changed the Colorado River. Many sections of this once wild and dangerous river have been tamed. The dams have also shrunk the river in size. Environmentalists feel that some of the dams should be closed and that the river should be allowed to return to its natural state.

Today

The Colorado River region is like no other place on Earth. Each year, more than 5 million people come from around the world to see the breathtaking views at the Grand Canyon and other area sites.

These unique natural treasures are in danger today. Some say that the Grand Canyon's popularity is causing problems. The many cars that bring tourists to the canyon contribute to a major park problem: air pollution.

In addition to car exhaust, air pollution from a nearby power plant is a problem at the Grand Canyon. On some days, the haze is so bad that visitors can't enjoy the canyon's magnificent (mag-NIH-fih-sent) scenery (SEEN-er-ee). Air pollution from cities near and far also clouds canyon views. At times, pollution from as far away as Phoenix, Arizona, or even Los Angeles (los AN-jell-ess), California, affects the park.

Noise pollution has also become a problem in the Grand Canyon area. In 2000, the Federal Aviation Administration (FAA) limited the number of airplane flights over the Grand Canyon. It also designated 75 percent of the park area as flight-free. The FAA hoped to reduce the amount of noise in the area by taking this step. The group hopes to restore "natural quiet" by 2008.

Many groups are working hard to preserve the Grand Canyon for future generations (jen-er-AY-shunz).

GRAND CANYON NATIONAL PARK

Known as the crown jewel of the national park system, Grand Canyon National Park was established in 1919 by President Woodrow Wilson. In the park's first year, 44,000 people visited the canyon. Today, more than 5 million people visit the park each year. The park covers more than 2 million acres (800,000 hectares) of land.

Visitors line the overlook at Mather Point in Grand Canyon National Park in Arizona.

The Grand Canyon Trust and the National Parks Conservation Association (uh-soh-see-AY-shun) are two such groups. These organizations work hard to educate people about the threats to the Grand Canyon and other national parks. They hope that once citizens learn more, they will take action to save the parks.

THEODORE ROOSEVELT AND THE GRAND CANYON

In 1903, President Theodore Roosevelt visited the Grand Canyon for the first time. He was awed by what he saw. Roosevelt called the canyon "one of the great sights that every American if he can travel at all should see." He urged Americans to preserve the canyon as it was. Roosevelt himself took steps to keep the canyon intact. In 1906, he established the Grand Canyon Game Reserve. Two years later, he designated the Grand Canyon as a national monument.

Great Plains

2

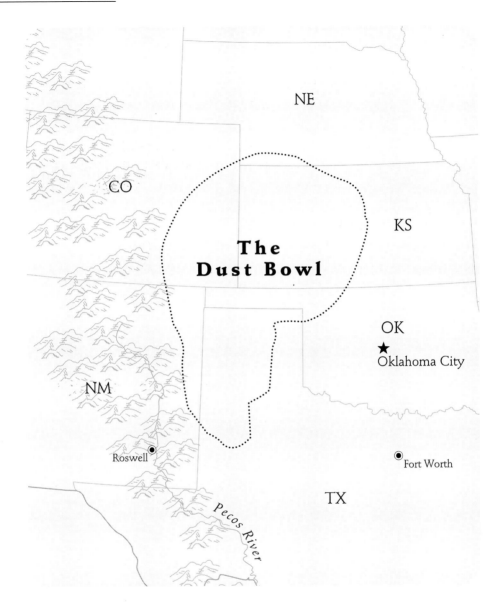

The Great Plains are a large grassy region that extends more than 2,500 miles (4,000 kilometers) from Canada in the north to Texas in the south. The western border of the Great Plains is the Rocky Mountains. The eastern border is near the 100th meridian of longitude (LAWN-jih-tood). The 100th meridian is an imaginary (ih-MAJ-in-er-ee) line that begins at the North Pole and runs south through the center of the United States to the South Pole. The width of the Great Plains varies from 300 miles (480 kilometers) in some areas to 700 miles (1,120 kilometers) in others. These vast, rolling grasslands stretch through parts of the Southwestern states of Oklahoma, New Mexico, and Texas, as well as ten other Western and Midwestern states.

The Great Plains region is *semiarid*, which means that it receives less than average rainfall each year. Generally (JEN-er-ul-lee), less than 20 inches (50 centimeters) of rain falls in the area each year. The plains are also subject to weather extremes. In the winter, blizzards and bitterly cold temperatures sweep the plains. In the summer, heat blisters the plains, and dust storms, tornadoes, and frequent thunderstorms can cause serious damage throughout the region.

In the Southwest, the Great Plains were some of the last lands to be settled by Americans. At first, the plains and prairies were the domain of Native American tribes. Slowly, however, the native peoples were pushed off their lands, and pioneers began forging new lives for themselves there. The plains are an important part of the region's—and the nation's— economy. The area is known for its agricultural and mineral wealth.

TALKING ABOUT THE PLAINS

Parts of the Great Plains in the Southwest are known as the *Llano Estacado* (YAH-noh es-tah-KAH-doh). The first name given to the area by early Spanish explorers, llano estacado means "staked plain" in Spanish. Some historians believe that the Spanish gave the area this nickname because they drove wooden stakes into the ground as they traveled. The stakes allowed the explorers to find their way back to where they had started. The llano, which includes parts of northeastern New Mexico and northwestern Texas, covers about 32,000 square miles (83,200 square kilometers).

The Pecos River, pictured here, was once known as the Río Salado (Salty River) because of its salty taste.

THE PECOS RIVER

One of the rivers that flows through the Great Plains is the Pecos River. The Pecos begins in New Mexico and flows for 926 miles (1,482 kilometers) until it reaches the Rio Grande in Texas. Carlsbad, New Mexico, and Pecos, Texas, are located along the river.

Settlement

Some of the earliest arrivals on the Great Plains of the Southwest were people who settled there more than 11,000 years ago. The first people believed to live in the area were the Clovis people. The Clovis hunted mammoths—ancient creatures related to elephants— and other big game in the area. Later groups included the Folsom and Plainview peoples. Just as later native tribes did, the Folsom and Plainview hunted bison, or buffalo, throughout the Southwestern plains.

The first Europeans to explore the area were the Spanish. In 1540, Francisco Vásquez de Coronado (fran-SISS-koh VAHS-kez deh kor-oh-NAH-doh) led an expedition of 300 men into the Southwestern plains. The Spaniards had heard that there were magnificent (mag-NIH-fih-sent) cities of gold somewhere in the region. Coronado was determined to discover them.

During Coronado's journey, the *conquistador* (kohn-KEESS-tah-dor), or "conqueror," wandered through the plains of New Mexico, Texas, and Oklahoma. His party traveled for 3,000 miles (4,800 kilometers), discovering the Grand Canyon and visiting several native villages along the way. However, they found absolutely no trace of gold or riches in the area.

After Coronado's expedition, the Spanish lost interest in the plains region. The officials (uh-FISH-uls) of New Spain (now Mexico) were interested only in gold. When they didn't find the treasures that they sought, they decided that the land of the Southwestern plains was useless. Nevertheless, Spanish adventurers and settlers in New Spain did have a profound effect on the Great Plains in the Southwest. The Spanish left behind horses. By the late 1600s, herds of wild horses were roaming the plains.

In the late 1600s and early 1700s, a number of tribes from the north migrated to the Southwestern plains to be closer to the herds of horses. The Kiowa (KYE-oh-wuh), Apache (uh-PATCH-ee), and Comanche (kuh-MAN-chee) peoples were among the earliest of these tribes. For a time, the Apache dominated the plains, hunting buffalo on horseback and raiding enemy tribes for any other items that they needed. To protect the less warlike tribes in the area, the Spanish set up missions where Native Americans could take refuge from the Apaches. The missions soon became raiding targets themselves.

• Fast Fact •

The highest point in Oklahoma is on the Great Plains. Black Mesa, the remains of an ancient lava flow, is 4,973 feet (1,492 meters) high.

During the late 1600s, the Comanche people began to migrate into the plains from the Great Basin area. The Comanches were even more warlike than the Apaches. They quickly became the enemies of the Apaches and eventually became the strongest tribe on the Southwestern plains.

Like the Apache, the Comanche's way of life centered on the horse. The Comanches roamed the plains on horseback, following the huge herds of buffalo. The buffalo were central to the Plains tribes' lifestyle. The tribes used buffalo meat for food. They used buffalo hides to make clothing, blankets, and tepees. The more important Comanche tribe members were, the more horses they owned.

Americans Arrive

The United States gained possession of the Oklahoma plains in 1803, after the Louisiana Purchase. France sold the United States 800,000 square miles (2.08 million square kilometers) from the Mississippi River west to the Rocky Mountains. The Louisiana Purchase doubled the size of the nation. Soon after the sale, government expeditions were sent to explore the new territory.

One of the first U.S. expeditions in the Southwestern Great Plains was led by Stephen Long. Long's trip was a disaster from the start. He thought that he was exploring the Red River, but he was actually on the Canadian River. Later, many of his notes and records of the trip were stolen. Long was so unimpressed with the region that he called it "the Great American Desert."

For years, most of the Southwest plains area was scorned by settlers. Westward-bound pioneers saw the plains as a hazard that had to be traveled across as quickly as possible. As adventurers, buffalo hunters, and settlers traveled into or through the Great Plains, tribes in the region began to feel threatened. The Comanches, for example, felt that the white travelers were intruding on their hunting grounds.

To discourage settlers, Comanches sometimes raided forts, trading posts, or wagon trains in the region. They stole horses, supplies, and even women and children during these lightning-fast strikes. In some cases, the women were married off to tribal members. Sometimes, kidnapped children were adopted by the tribe.

In May 1836, Comanches raided Fort Parker, Texas. Nine-year-old Cynthia Ann Parker was among the hostages taken during the raid. Cynthia spent the next twenty-four years living as a Comanche. She married a chief and had three children. One of her children, Quanah Parker, was the last great chief of the Comanches.

In 1860, Cynthia Parker was recaptured by the U.S. Army. She was taken to live with her uncle in Texas. Over the next few years of her life, she tried again and again to escape and return to the Comanches. Each time, she was caught and returned to her uncle. Cynthia Parker died in 1870.

The Shrinking "Indian Territory"

In the 1830s, the U.S. government began creating policies (PAHL-uh-seez) to move Native American tribes from the east to land west of the Mississippi. In 1830, the government passed the first of these policies, the Indian Removal Act. This act, and others that followed, required such tribes as the Cherokee, Choctaw, Chickasaw, Creek, and Seminole to be moved off their lands and relocated in "Indian Territory." In 1834, land set aside as Indian Territory included what is now Oklahoma, Kansas, and Nebraska.

Many of the native peoples did not want to leave their homelands. However, the wishes of the tribes were not important to the settlers who wanted the land for themselves. Native Americans who refused to go west were forcibly (FOR-suh-blee) escorted there by U.S. troops. During the 1830s, an estimated 70,000 native people were relocated to Indian Territory.

In 1838 and 1839, as many as 20,000 Cherokee were forced to make an 800-mile (1,280-kilometer) march from their tribal lands in Georgia to the plains. Locked up in military stockades, hundreds of people died before the march even started. Thousands more died along the way. Some starved or died from disease. During winter months, many froze to death. The march became known as the Trail of Tears.

Although the Native American tribes were promised that the Indian Territory would be theirs for "as long as the grass shall grow and rivers run," the promise was soon broken. In 1853, the Kansas-Nebraska Act allowed Americans to settle these two territories. Then in 1889, the government opened up western Oklahoma to homesteaders. In 1907, the Indian Territory—or what was left of it—became part of Oklahoma when the state was accepted into the Union.

The Plains Peoples Fight Back

During the 1800s, the Plains tribes also began losing their grip on their homelands. In the early 1850s, Texas officials began passing laws that sent Texas tribes, including the Comanche, to reservations throughout the state. In 1859, the federal government decided that the Comanche and other tribes would be sent to the Indian Territory in Oklahoma.

Some of the native people did not want to give up their land without a fight. Tribes that had once been enemies banded together to fight off the settlers. In

THE 1889 LAND RUN

On April 22, 1889, thousands of settlers waited anxiously (ANK-shuss-lee) at the border of the Oklahoma Territory. At the stroke of noon, the mad rush was on. Men and women raced across the border. They were in a hurry to lay claim to their share of nearly 3 million free acres (1.2 million hectares) being offered up to homesteaders by the U.S. government. Most people obeyed the rules and waited until noon to start the land run, but others didn't want to wait. They arrived early and staked out the best available lands for themselves. These people were dubbed "Sooners," because they arrived sooner than anyone else. Today, Oklahoma's nickname is "the Sooner State." The 1889 event was the first of several such land grabs that stripped most of the land away from Native Americans in the region. As more people settled in the region, towns and cities sprang up to serve them. Oklahoma City got its start as a tent city during the 1889 Land Run.

THE LAST CHIEF: QUANAH PARKER

The son of Cynthia Ann Parker and a Comanche (kuh-MAN-chee) chief, Quanah Parker fought hard to preserve the land and lifestyle of his people. Eventually, Parker was forced onto a reservation in Oklahoma with the rest of his tribe. Once there, Parker tried to adjust to his new life. He encouraged his people to make the best of their situation. Yet he also reminded them to keep the culture and traditions of the Comanche alive. Parker, a friend of President Theodore Roosevelt, died in 1911.

June 1874, Chief Quanah Parker of the Comanche led about 700 Comanche, Kiowa, and Cheyenne (SHYE-ann) warriors to a buffalo-hunting camp in Texas. Twenty-eight hunters were able to hold off the warriors until help arrived. The event sparked the Red River War (1874–1875), which led to the defeat of the Plains tribes. By the late 1870s, any remaining Plains tribes had been forced onto reservations in Oklahoma.

opposite:
The Comanche Chief Quanah Parker never lost a battle with the U.S. Army. Eventually, he surrendered and led his tribe to life on a reservation in Oklahoma.

To make sure that the native peoples could not return to the plains, the U.S. government encouraged hunters and troops to kill the buffalo herds there. Until the 1870s, millions of buffalo roamed the plains. The greatest number grazed in the Southwest. By 1878, however, the Southwestern buffalo had been nearly wiped out.

Tornado Alley

The United States is the world's tornado hot spot. More twisters touch down here than on any other place on Earth. In 2001, hundreds of tornadoes tore through the nation. Within the United States, the Great Plains of Oklahoma and Texas are part of a larger area that has been nicknamed "tornado alley." Tornadoes here are not uncommon, especially (es-PESH-ul-ee) during the months of April, May, and June.

A *tornado* is a violent, circling column of air that can result from a severe thunderstorm. A tornado sometimes forms a funnel-shaped cloud that reaches down to the ground. The funnel cloud acts like a vacuum, sucking up and smashing anything in its path. Tornadoes move along the ground at speeds from 5 to 30 miles (8 to 48 kilometers) per hour. However, the winds inside the funnel cloud can rage at up to 250 miles (400 kilometers) per hour. During one severe storm in 1878, a tornado picked up a cow and carried it 10 miles (16 kilometers).

Tornadoes can cause a great deal of damage in just a short time. Through the decades, towns on the plains have been torn apart by these massive storm systems. Twisters can also be deadly. In 2001, forty-eight people were killed by tornadoes in the United States. People who live on the Southwestern plains know that at the first hint of trouble, they must take cover. This means heading into a storm shelter or a basement and waiting until the storm has passed.

It is impossible for *meteorologists* (mee-tee-or-AHL-oh-jists), scientists who study the weather, to forecast tornadoes. However, many states in tornado-prone areas have developed tornado warning systems. These warning systems let people know when conditions are right for tornadoes to develop.

• Fast Fact •
The word tornado **is from the Spanish word** tronada, **or "thunderstorm."**

Commerce

The plains area, with its grassy flatlands, is the perfect place for raising and grazing livestock. Some of the earliest ranchers in the region were sheepherders on the New Mexico plains. Thousands of sheep were brought to New Mexico in the late 1590s by Spanish settlers. The Spanish settlers also brought along cattle.

Cattlemen began settling on the Texas plains in the 1860s. In 1876, Charles Goodnight established one of the first large ranches on the Texas plains. Home Ranch would eventually cover more than 1 million acres (400,000 hectares) and set hundreds of thousands of cattle out to graze. Goodnight also blazed a number of cattle trails from Texas to markets in the west and the north.

GREAT PLAINS TWISTERS

Tornadoes are serious disasters. Some of the most deadly and damaging of these disasters have occurred on the Great Plains. Here are a few of the worst.

- May 18, 1902: A tornado ripped through the town of Goliad, Texas, destroying everything in its path. The twister lasted just four minutes. During this short time, 114 people were killed.

- April 1947: Called the Woodward Tornado, this severe storm was actually six separate twisters. The storm traveled 221 miles (354 kilometers) across Texas, Oklahoma, and Kansas. It cut a trail of destruction 1.5 miles (2.4 kilometers) wide and left 181 people dead in its wake. The tornado was the most deadly in Oklahoma history.

- May 11, 1953: The Waco Tornado was Texas's worst tornado disaster. The powerful storm killed 114 people and injured more than 1,000. Damages exceeded $40 million.

- April 10, 1979: The Red River Valley Tornadoes were three twisters that swept through Texas and Oklahoma. The severe storms caused 56 deaths, more than 1,900 injuries, and $63 million in damages.

This modern-day cattle drive down the Rio Grande flood plain brings cattle to the Southwestern International Livestock Show and Rodeo.

Cattle drives were the chief way of getting the cows to market. Drives in the Southwest had taken place as early as the 1830s. At that time, cowboys herded wild, unbranded cattle to New Orleans. The head of cattle fetched a much higher price in that booming port city than they did in Texas.

Later, cattle were driven anywhere there was a market for beef. For example, cattle were driven to the gold fields of California, the mines of Montana, and the Native American reservations of New Mexico. Starting in the 1870s, the most important destinations included Dodge City and Abilene (AB-ih-leen), Kansas. Here the cattle were loaded onto railroad cars and shipped to Chicago, Illinois (il-ih-NOY), and other processing centers.

Cattle drives were long, often unpleasant trips. The journey from Texas sometimes covered hundreds of miles of rough, rugged terrain. Groups of cowboys would drive big herds of cattle over the plains, across raging rivers, and over mountains and hills. They faced Native American raiding parties, bad weather, and stampedes. Cowboys ate their dinners around campfires and slept outside under the stars.

In later years, a typical cattle drive could include 3,000 head of cattle being driven by eleven or twelve cowboys. Although the trips were long and difficult, they were also profitable for both the rancher and the cowboys. For example, a cow that sold for two dollars in Texas might sell for twenty times that in other markets.

• *Fast Fact* •

In the early days of the cattle industry, wild cows roamed freely throughout the plains. Cowboys called these cows *mavericks.* **They were free for the taking. To claim the cows as his own, a cowboy would** *brand,* **or burn, the mark of his ranch onto the cattle.**

Among the most important cattle trails were the Shawnee Trail from Austin, Texas, to Kansas City, Missouri; the Goodnight-Loving Trail from Young County, Texas, to Denver, Colorado; and the Western Trail from Bandera, Texas, to Dodge City, Kansas. However, the busiest trail out of Texas was the Chisholm (CHIZ-um) Trail. The Chisholm Trail stretched from San Antonio up through the Texas plains and into Oklahoma. Historians estimate that as many as 10 million head of cattle were driven over this trail.

LONGHORN CATTLE

Texas is famous for a special breed of cattle: the Texas longhorn. The longhorn developed when cattle left behind by Spanish settlers mixed with those brought by American settlers. The hardy longhorns were a favorite of cowboys on long cattle drives. They stayed very healthy and had super-hard hooves that held up well during the long trips.

Changing Times

The era of the big drives came to an end in the 1880s. Large corporations began buying up the smaller ranches scattered throughout the plains. They erected barbed-wire fencing to mark off their property and to keep their own herds of cattle safe. As people began more carefully fencing off their own property, cattle trails were often closed to drivers, too. Finally, the railroads extended into the Southwestern plains. The cattle no longer needed to be driven to railway hubs up north.

Another innovation that led to the end of cattle drives was refrigeration (ree-frij-er-AY-shun). As early as 1869, a refrigerated ship was used to take Texas beef to New Orleans. In the 1870s, cold cars for railroads were developed. This meant that Texas beef could now be transported around the nation without spoiling. Before long, slaughterhouses (SLAW-ter-how-sez) sprang up in Texas to process beef closer to home before shipping it.

Cattle ranching continues to play an important part in the plains economy. Today, Texas is the number-one cattle state in the nation. There are more than 15 million head of cattle in the state. Texas is also the top sheep and goat state.

Farming

The early 1880s were a time of heavy rainfall on the Southwestern Great Plains. Encouraged by the moist climate, more and more farmers began planting crops on the plains. Areas that had once been used for livestock grazing were now plowed and seeded with a variety of crops. Wheat and cotton were two of the biggest crops in the area. By the early 1900s, Texas was the number-one cotton-producing state in the nation.

EXODUSTERS

Exodusters were former slaves who headed to the Great Plains of Oklahoma and Kansas, looking for land of their own. The largest numbers arrived between 1870 and 1880, after the Civil War (1861–1865). In Oklahoma, many all-black towns were founded by groups of these settlers.

The people of the Southwestern plains were known as "dry farmers." They had no access to a constant supply of water. Instead, they depended entirely upon rain to nourish their crops. During the rainy years of the early 1880s, the farmers did well. However, the rain didn't last forever. The troubles of the plains farmers were just beginning.

Trouble in the Dust Bowl

In 1929, the rain stopped falling on the plains. The topsoil, ruined by years of plowing, dried up quickly. Then in the mid-1930s, things got even worse for the plains farmers. The wind began to blow. It blew hard. It lifted the topsoil into the air, creating huge clouds of dust that blackened the sky and covered everything for miles around. People began calling the windswept region the Dust Bowl.

• *Fast Fact* •

In the Dust Bowl, the massive dust storms of the 1930s became known as "black blizzards."

The dust was everywhere. It buried roads and piled up against houses and barns. Every day, farmers wiped the dust from the mouths and nostrils of their cows and other livestock. There was no escaping it. It seeped in through cracks in the walls and ceilings, covering beds, tables, and dishes. People, especially the very young and the very old, became sick from breathing in the dust. Some even died of "dust pneumonia" (noo-MOHN-ya), a lung condition caused by breathing too much dirt.

Thousands of acres of land throughout the plains were affected by the raging winds. The southern Great Plains were hit the hardest. Oklahoma, Texas, and New Mexico all suffered, as did parts of Kansas and Colorado. In all, 150,000 square miles (390,000 square kilometers) of land were affected.

One of the worst dust storms began on May 9, 1934. For three days, the winds blew. Millions of tons of topsoil were grabbed up by the wind and carried away. Some of the dust was blown all the way to New England and Washington, D.C. People everywhere now realized that something terrible was happening on the plains.

Farm equipment and buildings are buried under mounds of dust in this 1936 photograph of Guymon, Oklahoma.

THE GREAT DEPRESSION

The Great Depression was the worst economic crisis that the United States ever faced. It began in October 1929, when the stock market crashed. During the next decade, thousands of Americans lost their jobs, their homes, and their pride. Many lived on the streets, begging for money or standing in bread lines to get a meal. The Dust Bowl problems occurred during the worst years of the Depression.

The Mother Road

As the wind continued to blow year after year, it destroyed the hopes of those who lived on the plains. Thousands of families in the Southwest found that they could no longer keep their farms. Some farms were taken by the banks when the farmers couldn't keep up with the mortgage payments they owed. Other families just left the area, knowing that the future there was dim and hoping that it was brighter somewhere else.

The Dust Bowl disaster sparked the largest migration of people within the United States ever. Every day, hundreds of families packed up their few belongings and headed away from the plains. They left by car, train, and foot. Many of them were headed for the same destination: California.

For Dust Bowlers headed to California, the roadway of choice was Route 66. Following old trade paths, Route 66 stretched through New Mexico and Arizona before ending in Bakersfield, California. Migrants began calling the road "the Mother Road." Although the journey was long and difficult, many people made the trip. They heard that there was work and the promise of a better life in California. By the end of the 1930s, more than 2 million people had migrated out of the plains states.

THE GRAPES OF WRATH

In 1939, reporter John Steinbeck published *The Grapes of Wrath*. This book about a Dust Bowl family, the Joads, attracted attention around the nation. The story followed the Joads from their Oklahoma farm to a California work camp. The book won Steinbeck the Pulitzer Prize for fiction. The book was controversial, and some hated it. Many California officials (uh-FISH-uls) and farm owners banned and burned the book. Here is an excerpt.

And then the dispossessed were drawn west—from Kansas, Oklahoma, Texas, New Mexico; from Nevada and Arkansas [AR-ken-saw] families, tribes, dusted out, tractored out. Carloads, caravans, homeless and hungry; twenty thousand and fifty thousand and a hundred thousand and two hundred thousand. They streamed over the mountains, hungry and restless—restless as ants, scurrying to find work to do—to lift, to push, to pull, to pick, to cut—anything, any burden to bear, for food. The kids are hungry. We got no place to live. Like ants scurrying for work, for food, and most of all for land.

In California, however, many of the Dust Bowl migrants found nothing but poverty, discrimination, and despair. Because the greatest number of migrants came from Oklahoma, people in California began calling them "Okies." Having little or no money, the migrants were forced to live in camps that were not clean. Some camps didn't even have toilets. Some of the people who had survived the Dust Bowl and the long, grueling trip west died in the unhealthy camps of California.

After the Dust Bowl disaster, the U.S. government took steps to make sure that such a thing never happened on the plains again. Government agents taught farmers how to protect the land. The farmers learned how to rotate crops, leaving different fields empty each year while others were planted. Crop rotation preserves important organic matter in the soil, helping the land stay healthy and fertile. Another technique (tek-NEEK) to save the land was planting grass and trees to keep the topsoil in place.

Thanks to deep irrigation and better farming practices, wheat and cotton are now both grown extensively on the Southwestern Great Plains, as are hay and peanuts. Texas remains the top cotton state in the nation.

Petroleum on the Plains

An early gusher spews oil from the Glenn Pool area outside Tulsa, Oklahoma. The Glenn Pool was Oklahoma's first large oil field.

The Great Plains of the Southwest are well known for their mineral wealth. In Oklahoma, oil was discovered on the plains near Chelsea in 1889. A few years later, commercial (kuh-MER-shul) oil wells began gushing oil throughout the Oklahoma plains. As a result of the oil boom, Tulsa, Oklahoma, grew from a small farming town into a big city almost overnight. Before long, the city had earned the nickname "the oil capital of the world."

Oil caused many other plains towns to grow and prosper. Oklahoma City, where oil was struck in 1930, was one such town. The oil boom boosted Oklahoma's population and made it a good candidate for statehood. Plains oil is also important to the state of Texas. Oil was first discovered on the Texas plains in the 1920s.

Today

A major concern of Great Plains people today is water. Farmers, ranchers, and residents all need water to run their businesses and survive. However, the plains region receives less *precipitation* (pruh-sip-ih-TAY-shun), which is rain or snow, than many other areas in the nation. The plains receive an average of 10 to 30 inches of precipitation each year. By contrast, the Midwest receives from 20 to 40 inches, and the Southeast and Northeast receive about 40 to 60 inches of precipitation each year. The amount of rainfall becomes less on the plains from east to west. To conserve this important natural resource in drier years, local and state officials often ask residents to ration water.

Plains residents use local rivers, streams, and lakes as sources for irrigation and drinking water. Water is also found in *aquifers* throughout the region. An aquifer is a large underground source of water. One important aquifer that supplies water to the Southwestern Plains is the Ogallala Aquifer. Water from the Ogallala Aquifer is used to irrigate crops in Oklahoma and Texas.

Pollution is also a problem on the plains. Fertilizers and other chemicals (KEM-ik-ulz) from farms sometimes run into water supplies. Because water is so precious, people understand the importance of making sure that water supplies stay fresh and clean. Government and other agencies (AY-jen-seez) are looking for ways to halt Great Plains pollution.

This Oklahoma farmer plows his field with a three-horse team just as farmers throughout the Great Plains did when the region was first settled.

Although the region is sparsely settled, the Great Plains continue to play an important part in the Southwest's economy. The plains are still known for ranching, farming, and their mineral wealth.

Gulf of
Mexico

3

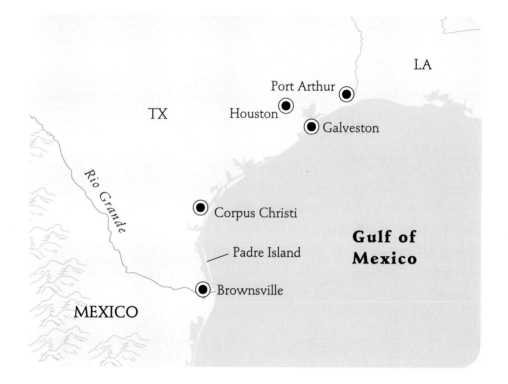

The Gulf of Mexico is a western arm of the Atlantic Ocean. It serves as the southeastern border of Texas. Covering nearly 600,000 square miles (1.6 million kilometers), it is the largest gulf in the world. The gulf is connected to the Atlantic Ocean by the Straits of Florida. The Yucatán (yook-uh-TAN) Channel to the south connects the gulf to the Caribbean (kaehr-ib-BEE-an) Sea.

The gulf coast of Texas measures about 370 miles (592 kilometers) from Brownsville to Sabine. Texas's gulf coast has a subtropical climate, with mild winters and very hot summers. As a result, the region is popular with vacationers. Hurricanes in the late summer and early fall are a serious threat along the coast.

The Gulf of Mexico played an important role in the exploration and settlement of Texas, as well as the Southeastern United States. Over the years, the coast has become an internationally important commercial (kuh-MER-shul) and industrial area. People around the world benefit from products that come from the gulf region. These products include oil, natural gas, chemicals (KEM-ik-ulz), manufactured goods, seafood, rice, and cotton.

Settlement

One of the first peoples to make their homes along the gulf coast were the Karankawa people. This Native American tribe lived in the area of what is now Texas, from Galveston to Corpus Christi. They roamed the gulf coastal plains, looking for deer, rabbit, and other animals. The Karankawa tribes also crafted dugout canoes (kuh-NOOZ) and took fish and shellfish from the gulf waters. Other important groups of Native Americans in the area were the Coahuiltec (koh-uh-WEE-tek) and the Atakapa.

COMPARING THE GULF

The Gulf of Mexico is a large but shallow body of water. Here's how it measures up against some other bodies of water throughout the world.

Body of Water	Size	Average Depth	Maximum Depth
Gulf of Mexico	596,000 sq. miles (1,549,600 sq. kilometers)	5,300 feet (1,590 meters)	14,200 feet (4,260 meters)
Caribbean Sea	1,063,000 sq. miles (2,763,800 sq. kilometers)	8,400 feet (2,520 meters)	25,200 feet (7,560 meters)
Bering Sea	876,000 sq. miles (2,277,600 sq. kilometers)	4,700 feet (1,410 meters)	13,800 (4,140 meters)
Hudson Bay	470,000 sq. miles (1,222,000 sq. kilometers)	420 feet (126 meters)	850 feet (255 meters)
North Sea	222,000 sq. miles (577,200 sq. kilometers)	310 feet (93 meters)	2,200 feet (660 meters)

European Arrival

The first Europeans to explore the Gulf of Mexico in the Southwest were the Spanish. In 1508, Spanish explorer Sebastián de Ocampo entered the gulf, sailing around the island of Cuba. Eleven years later, Spanish explorer Alonso Álvarez de Piñeda (AHL-vah-rez deh peen-YAY-dah) became the first European to sail up the gulf coast of Texas. Piñeda named the bay that would one day become the site of one of the gulf's busiest ports: Corpus Christi (KRIS-tee). He also claimed the region for Spain.

NATURAL STORM PROTECTION

Seventeen barrier islands line the gulf coast of Texas. These barrier islands give the coast some protection from storms and hurricanes. The islands include Galveston, Matagorda, Brazos, Mustang, and Padre. Padre Island is the nation's largest barrier island. It is about 110 miles (176 kilometers) long and 3 miles (4.8 kilometers) wide.

In 1528, a Spanish expedition on its way back from Florida was wrecked on a barrier island off Texas's gulf coast. Among the handful of survivors was Álvar Núñez Cabeza de Vaca (AHL-var NOON-yez kah-BAY-sah deh VAH-kah). Cabeza de Vaca and his friends were probably the first nonnatives to set foot on the gulf coast in the Southwest. He and three other survivors returned to Mexico nine years later with wild stories of golden cities filled with treasure.

Over the next 100 years, the Spanish sent many exploratory parties into the Gulf of Mexico and Texas. During this time, most Spanish settlement took place along the southern coast, in Mexico. During the 1500s and 1600s, the gulf waters were considered Spanish property. Explorers from other nations stayed away.

Álva Núñez Cabeza de Vaca, the Spanish explorer, is shown trekking across the desert in the American Southwest.

This changed, however, in 1685. In February, French explorer René-Robert Cavelier (kav-ul-YAY), sieur (lord) de La Salle, established Fort St. Louis near Matagorda Bay on the gulf coast. La Salle and more than 200 colonists had arrived there by accident: They were searching for the mouth of the Mississippi River. Over the next two years, La Salle explored the surrounding regions, looking for the Mississippi. In 1687, he was murdered by his own men. Within three years, his settlement was destroyed by the Karankawa people.

The Spanish learned of La Salle's arrival on the Texas coast shortly after he landed. They were very upset. They wanted the French out of their territory. Spanish interest in the upper gulf coast revived. The Spanish began sending exploratory parties north, looking for the French. However, Spanish settlement along the coast was stalled by the fierce Karankawa tribe.

• Fast Fact •

Shortly after its founding in 1816, Galveston was taken over by pirate Jean Lafitte. Under Lafitte, the island became a center for smugglers and pirates. Lafitte controlled Galveston for nearly three years.

American Settlement

In the early 1800s, Americans began settling along the gulf coast of Texas. One early settlement was Galveston, founded in 1816 on Galveston Island. In 1835, Galveston played an important role when Texas fought to win its independence (in-duh-PEN-dense) from Mexico. In 1836, the city served briefly as the capital of the Texas Republic. During the Civil War (1861–1865), Galveston was a key shipping port for the Confederates. As such, it was a target for Union troops.

Jean Lafitte was a Louisiana privateer and smuggler who helped the United States forces in the Battle of New Orleans during the War of 1812.

Another coastal town that was settled by the Americans in the early 1800s was Corpus Christi. Corpus Christi was founded in 1838 as a trading post by Henry Lawrence Kinney. In 1845, U.S. general Zachary Taylor brought his troops to Corpus Christi before the Mexican War (1846–1848). After Taylor's arrival, the small outpost began to grow. By the early 1860s, Corpus Christi had become an important port. During the Civil War, it became a target for Union troops. In November 1863, the city was captured by the Union army.

This painting of General Sam Houston shows him as the first governor of the state of Texas.

SAM HOUSTON

Sam Houston (HYOO-stin) was a leader in Texas's battle for independence (in-duh-PEN-dense). In April 1836, Houston defeated Mexican troops at the Battle of San Jacinto (hah-SIN-toh). He was later named the first president of the new Republic of Texas. When Texas was made a state in 1845, Houston went to Washington as its first senator. Fourteen years later, he was elected governor of Texas. When state lawmakers voted to secede from the Union and join the Confederates in 1861, Houston stood firm against them. He refused to take an oath of allegiance (uh-LEE-jense) to the Confederacy. Houston was removed from office. He died two years later.

The largest city in the gulf coastal region—and in the state of Texas—is Houston (HYOO-stin). Houston got its start in 1836, founded by two brothers. Augustus and John Allen named their new settlement for Texas leader Sam Houston. Many of Houston's first settlers were from the Southeastern region of the United States. As a result, the town was strongly Confederate during the Civil War.

• Fast Fact •

The San Jacinto (hah-SIN-toh) Monument in Houston marks the spot where Texas won its final battle for independence (in-duh-PEN-dense) from Mexico on April 21, 1836.

Hurricanes and Other Disasters

Fierce storms and hurricanes are common along the gulf coast. During hurricane season, from late June through October, coastal residents pay careful attention to the weather forecasts. At the first sign of danger, people living along the coast must take precautions or evacuate. Galveston is especially (es-PESH-ul-ee) at risk from tropical storms. Since the 1800s, the island city has been battered and severely damaged a number of times.

One of the first recorded tropical storms in the gulf occurred in 1554. That year, four Spanish ships on their way from New Spain (Mexico) to Cuba were caught in a brutal gulf storm. Three of the ships were wrecked on Padre Island, and more than 150 men were killed in the disaster. In 1967, the remains of one of the ships, the *Espíritu Santo*, were discovered. Many valuable items were recovered from the wreck. A second wreck, the *San Esteban*, was discovered a few years later.

DISASTER AT TEXAS CITY

In 1947, an explosion on a ship in Texas City's
harbor set fire to other ships in the harbor.
More explosions followed, and the fire spread
to the docks. More than 500 people
were killed in the disaster.

GULF HURRICANES THROUGH THE CENTURIES

From 1527 onward, the Gulf of Mexico has been affected
regularly by deadly storms and hurricanes. Here are examples
from each century.

- November 1590: More than 1,000 people died at sea
  when nearly 100 ships went down during this big gale.
  This was one of the worst *maritime*, or ocean-related, disasters in history.

- October 21, 1631: Three hundred lives were lost at sea
  during a late-season hurricane.

- September 4, 1766: A hurricane hit Galveston Island. A
  mission on the mainland, San Augustine de Ahumado,
  was destroyed.

- *Racer's* Storm, October 2, 1837: Named for a ship that
  encountered the storm before it reached the gulf, this
  hurricane lasted for four days. At its fiercest, it beached
  ships and damaged property along the southern coast of
  Texas. The storm destroyed nearly every building on the
  island of Galveston.

- Hurricane Carla, September 14, 1961: Hurricane Carla was
  one of the strongest hurricanes in recorded time, second
  only to the Great New England Hurricane of 1938. Carla
  had winds that measured up to 175 miles (280 kilometers)
  per hour and raised coastal water levels to 22 feet
  (6.6 meters) in height. The super-strong storm caused more
  than $400 million in damages. Thirty-four people were killed.

One of the worst natural disasters to hit the gulf coast took place in 1900. That September, a wild hurricane blew into Galveston. Winds of about 120 miles (192 kilometers) per hour battered the coast, and high seas flooded the entire island of Galveston. About 8,000 people were killed by the storm. The 1900 hurricane remains the deadliest hurricane in U.S. history.

After the 1900 hurricane, Galveston erected a seawall for added protection against future storms. A *seawall* is a tall embankment to keep waves from battering the shore. The Galveston seawall is 10 miles (16 kilometers) long and 17 feet (5.1 meters) above the low-tide level. Corpus Christi also has a seawall.

Hurricanes will continue to batter the gulf coast. Strong recent hurricanes include Hurricane Alicia in 1983 and Hurricane Bret in 1999. Although Bret had winds of more than 110 miles (176 kilometers) per hour, its full force hit areas that had few residents and caused little serious damage.

Commerce

Two important industries along the gulf coast make use of the area's natural resources: farming and fishing. Citrus, cotton, and vegetables are all grown along the coast. A major coastal crop is rice, which is grown in the marshy regions near the coast. Rice farming began in the 1850s. In the 1880s, rice from coastal Texas was loaded onto railroad cars and carried around the nation. By the early 1900s, Texas rice was being shipped throughout the world.

A major development occurred in the rice industry in 1904. That year, Houston businessmen invited Japanese rice farmers to visit Texas. The Japanese farmers brought bags full of rice seed to the United States. The seed, a gift from Japan's emperor, produced greater amounts of rice than local seed did. Soon, Texas rice farmers began importing rice seed from Japan to increase their crop production.

The shrimp boat, Little David II, works close to the shore near Galveston, Texas.

Fishing is another key industry along the coast. Fishers take flounder, menhaden, and other types of fish out of the gulf. The most important seafood product, however, is shrimp. Ninety percent of all seafood taken from the gulf is shrimp. Shrimping on a large scale was begun after World War II (1939–1945). That's when shrimpers from Louisiana migrated to the gulf coast of Texas, looking for new territory.

Shipping

The gulf coast has a number of excellent (EK-sell-ent) deepwater ports that are used for trade and shipping. One of the first was Galveston. Other important Texas ports include Houston, Corpus Christi, Port Isabel, Texas City, Beaumont (BOH-mahnt), and Freeport. Houston is one of the busiest ports in the nation.

Shipping has been a major gulf industry since the early 1800s. In those early days, goods from settlements further inland were sent by wagon to Galveston, the number-one port on the coast. From there, they were shipped to New Orleans, Louisiana, where they were sold and shipped around the world. Items shipped out of the area included cotton, corn, and animal hides.

Some of the gulf's key ports became important only after improvements were made to them. In 1914, for example, the Houston Ship Channel was opened for business. The channel connected Houston to Galveston Bay, and the town quickly grew into an important shipping port. In 1926, Corpus Christi became a booming port when a channel to the gulf was deepened so large, oceangoing ships could get in and out.

By 1954, shipping had made the gulf coast one of the most commercially important areas in the nation. Petroleum, natural gas, and chemicals were all shipped out of gulf ports in large amounts. The completion of the Gulf Intracoastal Waterway in 1949 also boosted the shipping industry. This 1,100-mile (176-kilometer) canal connects the major ports along the gulf coast from Brownsville, Texas, to Fort Myers, Florida. Each year, about 80 million tons (72 million metric tons) of goods are transported along the waterway.

Oil and Other Minerals

In 1901, the discovery of oil near Beaumont, Texas, changed the state's economy forever. In January, a well in the Spindletop oil field began gushing the thick, black liquid from deep within the earth. The well gushed for nine days straight before workers found a way to cap it.

Thanks to Spindletop, Texas became the world's largest oil producer. A number of the big oil companies had their beginnings at Beaumont, including Texaco, Gulf, and Exxon. Since the discovery of oil in 1901, more than 150 million barrels of oil have been taken from the Beaumont oil field. Production at the field began to dwindle in the 1980s. Although Texas has lost its ranking as a world leader in oil production, it continues to be the top oil-producing state in the nation.

The Lucas gusher at Spindletop, Texas blows oil 200 feet into the air during the days immediately following the initial 1901 blowout.

Cities and towns in the surrounding areas boomed with the oil business. Gulf port cities grew rapidly, becoming the headquarters for oil storage, refining, and shipping. One city that especially benefited from the Spindletop well was Houston. Because of its inland location, Houston provided a safe shelter from hurricanes and wild gulf weather. For this reason, many oil barons chose to locate their headquarters and storage facilities here.

Another city that benefited from the oil boom was Corpus Christi. Soon, refineries, smelting plants, and chemical factories were being built there. In 1913, the discovery of natural gas in the area also boosted the city's economy. Today, Corpus Christi is a center for Texas's petroleum and petroleum-chemical industry.

ONE OF THE WORLD'S WORST SPILLS

Each year, about 1,000 oil spills—both large and small—occur on the gulf coast of Texas. The second-largest oil spill ever to occur in the world took place in the Gulf of Mexico on June 3, 1979. That year, an underwater oil well ruptured off the coast of Mexico, dumping 140 million gallons (532 million liters) of oil into the gulf. The oil reached the Texas coast in two months, killing fish and other sea life and polluting beaches. For years after the spill, gulf storms would wash oil and tar balls ashore onto Texas beaches.

THE CONTINENTAL SHELF

The Gulf of Mexico covers a gently sloping piece of Earth's crust known as the *continental shelf*. The continental shelf is the underwater edge of a continent. Waters above the shelf are shallow. Along the gulf coast, the continental shelf extends from 25 to 200 feet (7.5 to 60 meters) away from the shoreline before plunging into deeper ocean waters. Because of the shallow waters, the gulf floor can more easily be mined for oil, natural gas, and other underground resources.

Tourism

Tourism is another key coast industry. Because of the gulf's temperate climate, people from around the world vacation here year-round. They come to enjoy the fun and sun on gulf coast beaches, which by law are open to the public. Other tourists prefer the quiet of Padre Island National Seashore, off the coast of Corpus Christi.

Some people come to visit the home base of the National Aeronautics (ayr-oh-NAHT-iks) and Space Administration (NASA). Located in Houston, the Lyndon B. Johnson Space Center is NASA's top site for designing and testing spacecraft. Manned U.S. space flights are monitored from Houston's Mission Control Center.

Today

Pollution is a problem in the Gulf of Mexico. Trash and pollutants enter the gulf from a number of different sources. Fertilizers, pesticides (PESS-tih-sydez), and sewage, for example, are carried into the gulf by the two big rivers that empty into it: the Mississippi and the Rio Grande. Oil rigs and ships that dump garbage and waste pollute gulf waters. Even the gulf coast's popularity poses problems. Today, nearly 5 million people live near the coastline. This increased population has placed more stress upon the coast and surrounding environments. As houses, shops, and other buildings are built in the region, fewer wild areas remain. Of course, an increase in people means an increase in pollution.

opposite:
A group of visitors walks beneath the Apollo spacecraft at NASA's Johnson Space Center in Houston, Texas.

FAMOUS GULF COASTERS

Some famous folk were born on the gulf coast of Texas. Here are just a few.

- Famous 1960s singer Janis Joplin was born in Port Arthur.

- Howard Hughes, the eccentric (ek-SEN-trik) billionaire, was born in Houston. He made his money leasing oil-drilling equipment.

- Dan Rather, the CBS news anchor, hails from Wharton.

- Born in Port Arthur, super-athlete Mildred "Babe" Didrikson Zaharias earned two Olympic gold medals in 1932. She later became a champion golfer.

Over the years, people in the area have been working to keep the gulf and its coastline clean. In 1973, an international treaty called MARPOL made dumping oil, chemicals, sewage, and other garbage from oil rigs and ships illegal. Coastal community members pitch in, too. Twice a year, Texans clean up their beaches during the Adopt-a-Beach event. Since 1986, thousands of volunteers have cleaned up more than 4,000 tons (3,600 metric tons) of trash off the gulf coast shoreline.

Red River

4

Measuring nearly 1,220 miles (1,952 kilometers) from its headwaters to its mouth, the Red River is one of the longest rivers in the United States. The river's headwaters are in Curry County, New Mexico. The river then flows east into Texas. At Vernon, Texas, the Red River officially (uh-FISH-ul-ee) begins where the North Fork and the Prairie Dog Town Fork of the Red River join together. It flows east through Texas and continues along the Texas-Oklahoma border for 540 miles (864 kilometers). Once out of the Southwest, the Red River turns south, flowing through Arkansas (AR-ken-saw) and Louisiana until it ends in the Mississippi River.

The Red River has long been an important landmark in the Southwest. Since the early 1800s, the river has served as a boundary. In the past, the Red River separated French and Spanish territory in the region. Later, it marked the boundary between the

United States and Mexican territory. Today, it separates Texas from parts of Oklahoma and Arkansas.

Tributaries of the Red River—smaller rivers and streams that flow into it—include the Pease, Wichita, Sulphur, and Washita. The river drains more than 30,000 square miles (78,000 square kilometers) in Texas. It is one of two major rivers that drain the state of Oklahoma (the Arkansas River is the second). Important Red River towns in the Southwest include Wichita Falls, Texarkana, and Denison in Texas, and Marietta and Durant in Oklahoma.

Settlement

When Europeans arrived in the Red River area, they found several tribes living there. In the Southwest, a number of Caddoan-speaking (KAD-a-wan) tribes made their homes in Texas and Oklahoma. The Caddoan-speaking peoples were a group of tribes that lived in the Red River region. Caddoan-speaking tribes included the Pawnee, Nasoni (nuh-SOH-nee), and Arikara (uh-RIK-uh-ruh). The Caddo people were an important Caddoan-speaking tribe. They planted crops in the fertile soil along the banks of the river.

WHAT'S IN A NAME?

The Red River was called *Río Rojo,* or "Red River," by early Spanish explorers. During flooding, the river takes on a reddish tint when mineral-laden soil is washed into the water. When Americans began settling the region, they called the stream "the Red River of the Cadodacho," for the Caddo tribe. Today, the river is sometimes called the Red River of the South to distinguish it from the Red River of the North in the Midwest.

• Fast Fact •
The name *Texas* **comes**
from the Caddo word
tejas, **meaning**
"friend" or "ally."

Another Caddoan-speaking group was the Wichita (WICH-i-tah). The Wichita people first lived on the Great Plains of Kansas and Oklahoma. In the 1700s, the group was forced into the Red River region of Texas by the Osage people. In addition to farming, the Wichita also traded with other tribes in the area. They traded vegetables to the other tribes for horses. Then they traded the horses to European explorers for other supplies.

Another important group of Native Americans in the region were the Comanche (kuh-MAN-chee). The Comanche, unlike the Caddo, were nomadic. They roamed the plains and the Red River area on horseback, following herds of buffalo. The Comanche raided Caddoan villages and European and American settlements alike, taking food, horses, and anything else they needed. Other tribes who hunted and roamed through the area were the Kiowa (KYE-oh-wuh), Cheyenne (SHYE-ann), and Apache (uh-PATCH-ee).

• Fast Fact •
The Red River is very salty. Salt seeps into the river
from nearby salty springs and salt flats, adding
more than 3,000 tons (2,700 metric tons)
of salt to the water each day.

European Arrival

The first European to explore the Southwest Red River region was Spanish adventurer Francisco Vásquez de Coronado (fran-SISS-koh VAHS-kez deh kor-oh-NAH-doh). In 1541, Coronado explored the upper Prairie Dog Town Fork. He was the first nonnative person to see any part of the Red River.

In 1682, French explorer René-Robert Cavelier (kav-ul-YAY), sieur (lord) de La Salle, claimed

This undated engraving shows La Salle claiming the Mississippi Valley for France. La Salle's claim included the Red River and the entire Louisiana Territory.

Oklahoma as part of the Louisiana Territory for France. French explorers were soon trapping and trading along the river. They traded with the Caddo tribes in the area.

The Red River became the boundary between French and Spanish territory. The Spanish considered the land south of the Red River theirs. For the next 100 years, the Spanish would monitor French actions above the Red River very carefully.

The artist Thomas Scully painted this portrait of President Thomas Jefferson in 1821.

Whose Land?

In 1803, President Thomas Jefferson completed the Louisiana Purchase with France. The purchase gave the United States 800,000 square miles (2.08 million square kilometers) of land between the Rocky Mountains and the Mississippi River. The purchase included what is now the state of Oklahoma. Jefferson was eager to explore his new territory, including the Red River. He sent out a number of expeditions to explore the river and find its headwaters, or source.

One of the first U.S. expeditions along the river was led by Dr. John Sibley in 1803. Sibley provided the first detailed descriptions of the region. He also gained valuable information about the tribes living along the river.

In 1806, astronomer and surveyor Thomas Freeman led the first major scientific (sye-en-TIFF-ik) expedition of the river. Freeman's goal was to find the headwaters of the Red River. Freeman and his group followed the river up through Louisiana for more than 600 miles (960 kilometers). When they reached the border of Oklahoma and Texas, they were met by a troop of Spanish soldiers. The Spanish did not agree that the Red River was part of U.S. territory. They considered the land theirs, and they ordered the expedition to leave.

In 1852, Randolph B. Marcy and George McClellan set out to discover the source of the Red River. The two U.S. Army captains led a group of seventy men up the Red River. They continued up the Prairie Dog Town Fork, which they decided was the Red's main tributary and source. They charted previously unexplored land and discovered important mineral deposits in the region.

A year after the expedition, Marcy published his journal. The book sparked interest in the area, and the number of settlers to the Red River area increased. Marcy also published the first dictionary of Wichita words.

• Fast Fact •

During the Red River expedition of 1852, Marcy came upon a prairie dog town that covered 400,000 acres (160,000 hectares).

Americans Settle In

Thirteen years after Freeman's confrontation with the Spanish troops, Spain and the United States finally settled the conflict. In 1819, the two governments signed the Adams-Onís Treaty. According to the treaty, the boundary between the two nations was the Red River and the 100th meridian of longitude (LAWN-jih-tood). The 100th meridian is an imaginary (ih-MAJ-in-er-ee) line that begins at the North Pole and runs south through the center of the United States to the South Pole.

• Fast Fact •
The Adams-Onís Treaty was negotiated for the United States by future president John Quincy Adams.

In 1821, Mexico—now independent from Spanish rule—allowed Americans to settle in Texas. The Red River became a highway for settlers who flocked into the region. Others came from the north, crossing the river at spots that included Rock Bluff, Doan's Crossing, and Colbert's Ferry, Texas. The river also served as a pathway for miners working their way to the gold fields of California. One trail used by pioneers to cross the river into Texas was the Shawnee Trail, which had got its start as a cattle trail.

Americans who settled and hunted in the region often came to blows with area tribes. Comanche, Kiowa, and Apache groups in particular often raided U.S. settlements and buffalo-hunting camps. In 1845, the U.S. government began building the first of a string of forts that stretched from the Red River to the Rio Grande. However, tribal raiding parties had no difficulty avoiding the forts, and they continued to attack settlements south of the Red River.

This photograph, taken in 1862, shows General George McClellan when he was Commander-in-Chief of the Union armies.

GEORGE B. McCLELLAN

After he explored the Red River in 1852, George B. McClellan's career was on the rise. At the outset of the Civil War (1861–1865), "Little Mac" was appointed commander-in-chief of the Union army by President Abraham Lincoln. Lincoln soon became unhappy with his top officer, however. The president felt that McClellan was not aggressive enough, and he removed the general from his post. A bitter McClellan ran against Lincoln in the presidential election of 1864, but was beaten in a land-slide. McClellan later served as governor of New Jersey.

The Red River War

The mid-1800s saw an increasing number of people heading into the Red River region and onto the nearby plains. Native American tribes who had lived in the region for many years were pushed off their lands. Tribes such as the Comanche and Kiowa, who had depended upon the buffalo for survival, now watched as buffalo hunters slaughtered the animals by the thousands.

To make matters worse, the U.S. government passed the Indian Removal Act in 1830. President Andrew Jackson began sending Native American tribes to live in "Indian Territory"—what is now the state of Oklahoma. Any tribe that was living on land desired by Americans was resettled in Indian

Native American tribes such as the Comanche and Kiowa depended upon the American buffalo for food, clothing, and other essentials of life.

VOICES FROM THE PAST

Here are two different statements describing the opposing attitudes that led up to the Red River War (1874–1875).

> In our intercourse with the Indians it must always be borne in mind that we are the most powerful party.... We are assuming, and I think with propriety, that our civilization [siv-ih-luh-ZAY-shun] ought to take the place of their barbarous habits. We therefore claim the right to control the soil they occupy, and we assume it is our duty to coerce [koh-ERSE] them, if necessary [NESS-ess-err-ee], into the adoption and practice of our habits and customs.

This statement, by Secretary of the Interior Columbus Delano in his Annual Reports of 1872 and 1873, is typical of how many U.S. officials of the time thought about Native Americans. Delano talks about the native peoples as barbarians who should be pushed off their land and forced to adopt the ways of white Americans.

> I have kept out on the plains because the whites were bad. Now you come here to do good, you say, and the first thing you want to do is pen us up in a narrow territory. Ugh! I would rather stay out on the plains and eat dung than come in on such conditions.

As shown in this speech at the Alvord Council in 1872, Comanche (kuh-MAN-chee) Chief Tabananica (Sound of the Sun), like other Native Americans, wanted only to keep his tribal lands. Life on a reservation did not appeal to him.

Territory. The Chickasaw, Choctaw, Cherokee, Creek, and Seminole of the Southeast were ordered here, as were several smaller tribes.

The push to remove the Plains tribes to Indian Territory began in the 1870s. Some native groups, including the Cheyenne and the Arapaho (uh-RAP-uh-hoh), moved willingly into Indian Territory. Once they were there, they found buffalo hunters wiping out the herds that they needed to survive. The U.S. government promised to supply the tribes with food, but little arrived. The reservation groups faced starvation and sickness.

Along with Comanche and Kiowa groups, some Cheyenne and Arapaho warriors decided to fight back. The unhappy tribes banded together in a final effort to hold onto their lands and their lifestyle. Soon, Comanche chief Quanah Parker and others were leading raiding parties on American settlements and hunting camps.

At the end of July 1874, the U.S. government decided to end the Native American raiding near the river once and for all. The resulting battles between U.S. troops and bands of Plains warriors became known as the Red River War (1874–1875), because much of the fighting took place along the river.

In November 1874, U.S. forces attacked a Comanche camp, completely destroying the tribe's winter supplies and shelter. Without these, the remaining Native Americans were forced to seek shelter on the reservations in Indian Territory. Although small battles continued throughout the winter, the war was over. The tribes that had roamed the Red River region were now gone, confined to the Indian Territory. The last of the Plains tribes were on the reservations by June 1875.

State versus State

Disputes over the Red River boundary between Texas and Oklahoma have been going on for decades. The disputes often center on which tributary of the Red River is its main source—and therefore the border between the two states. In 1896, there was a boundary dispute between the Republic of Texas and the United States. The U.S. Supreme Court ruled that the Republic of Texas must give more than 1.5 million acres (600,000 hectares) to the United States. The land eventually became part of Oklahoma.

Twenty-five years later, oil was discovered in the bed of the Red River. Both Oklahoma and Texas claimed the find as their own. Before long, state troops on both sides were facing off across the river. Eventually, the U.S. Supreme Court once again stepped in. The court ironed out the problem, but not before a bridge had been burned and some mining equipment destroyed.

The most recent boundary battle between the two states ended in 2000. Both states had already agreed that the south bank was the official boundary. However, there was still some question about exactly where the south bank started. The particular spot in question was the Lake Texoma boundary. Lake Texoma is an important lake that spans the Red River in Texas and Oklahoma. In July 2000, the two states finally came to an agreement.

DENISON DAM AND LAKE TEXOMA

Denison Dam was built in 1944 to control flooding and create electrical energy on the Red River. The dam uses two big turbines to turn the power of falling water into electricity. A *turbine* is an engine containing a wheel with paddles, blades, or buckets. A turbine can be powered by flowing water, steam, or air.

The construction of Denison Dam created Lake Texoma, which is shared by both Texas and Oklahoma. Lake Texoma is a major recreational area that attracts millions of tourists each year. Visitors enjoy hunting, fishing, boating, and other activities in the Texoma area.

Commerce

One of the most important industries along the Red River is farming. Farming has been carried out along the river since Native Americans lived in the region. Later, settlers grew such crops as cotton, wheat, and vegetables. Cotton was one of the first crops grown by early American settlers along the river in Texas. It continues to be a major crop in both Texas and Oklahoma. Wheat is also still a key crop in the region, as are peanuts and vegetables. Timber and petroleum are important industries along the Red River today, as well.

Trade and Travel

In the early 1800s, a big obstacle stood in the way of boating on the Red River. This obstacle was a huge clump of trees and driftwood that clogged the river between Louisiana and Texas. (*Driftwood* is any piece of wood carried along by water.) Known as "the great Red River raft," the clump stretched for more than 160 miles (256 kilometers). Only canoes (kuh-NOOZ) could get through the mess.

In 1833, Captain Henry Miller Shreve decided to do something about this big bundle of brush and vegetation. He invented special battering-ram vessels and began to clear away the debris (duh-BREE). After six years, Shreve had destroyed the great raft, and trade took off on the Red River.

With the raft cleared, boats could travel for about 1,600 miles (2,560 kilometers) upriver from the port of New Orleans. As settlers began using the river to reach the West, trading posts sprang up at important river crossings. Some of the earliest were built in 1836. Traders running the posts traded with local natives and sold supplies to settlers crossing the Red River. They also used the river to transport goods from Texas to

opposite:
A farmer harvests wheat in a field near Okeene, Oklahoma. Wheat is an important commercial crop in the Red River area.

Louisiana. Cotton, vegetables, and other items floated between the two states. For a time, the Red River was the most important trade route in Texas.

THE GREAT RAFT RETURNS

Although Captain Henry Shreve got rid of the great Red River raft in the 1830s, people did not keep the Red River clear. By 1856, another big logjam of trees and driftwood had piled up in the same area. The raft was back! After this, river residents learned their lesson. The second great raft was cleared for good in 1874, and the river has been kept clear since then.

Cattle Drives

Starting in the 1830s, ranchers and cowboys drove huge herds of cattle from the Texas plains to railway stations and other destinations to the north. The cattle drives to the Red River were long trips that stretched over many miles of difficult terrain. Cowboys could earn a good wage on these drives, but they worked hard for every penny.

For many cattle drivers, the Red River was the last big obstacle on the trip. Crossing the Red could be very dangerous, for drivers and cattle alike. During flood season, the river could be wild and unpredictable. *Quicksand*—soft, soggy, unstable sand that could suck down a person or cow—was also a problem along the Red.

Several major cattle trails crossed the Red River. The most famous and well-used cattle trail of all, the Chisholm (CHIZ-um) Trail, was one of these. The Chisholm Trail crossing was at Red River Station, a small town in Montague County, Texas. The town grew and prospered as a result of the hundreds of cow herders who passed through on their way into Oklahoma Territory.

Another important cattle trail that crossed the Red was the Western Trail. The trail crossed the Red River at the site of an ancient buffalo trail near Vernon, Texas. The town of Doan's Crossing was built to serve the cattle drivers who were passing through. At its height, the town had 300 residents, as well as a hotel, a general (JEN-er-ul) store, and a saloon.

In 1873, crossing the Red became a lot easier for the cattle drivers. That year, the Missouri-Kansas-Texas railroad spanned the Red River at Colbert's Ferry. Eventually, the railroad would replace the long cattle drives. Little towns that had depended upon the cattle drives, including Red River Station and Doan's Crossing, slowly dried up and disappeared.

Today

People who live near the Red River know that it is a natural treasure. In 1955, the four states that have an interest in the river (Texas, Oklahoma, Arkansas, and Louisiana) formed the Red River Compact Commission (RCC). In addition to making sure the river and its waters are shared by all four states, the RCC works to protect the river for future generations (jen-er-AY-shunz).

Archaeologists work from a floating platform as they examine the remains of a steamboat that sunk in the Red River in 1838.

In recent years, the Army Corps of Engineers (en-jin-EERZ) has worked to control salt levels in the Red River. The engineers have constructed dams, as well as plants that collect and dispose of salt. The goal of the project is to remove some of the salt from the river in order to make the water drinkable.

Rio Grande

5

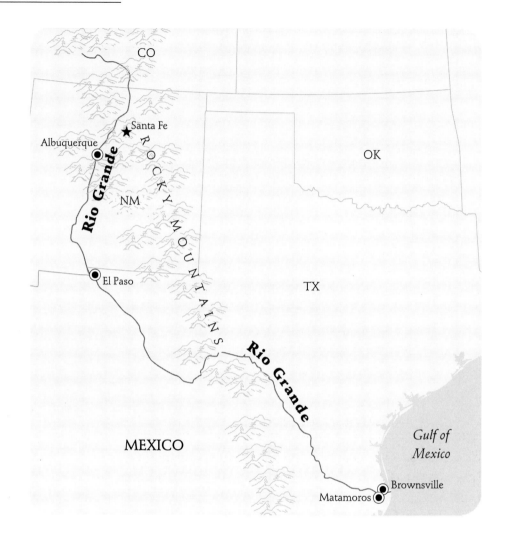

The Rio Grande is one of the longest rivers in the United States. It has its source in the San Juan Mountains of southwest Colorado. The San Juan Mountains are part of the Rocky Mountain Range. From here, the Rio Grande flows more than 1,880 miles (3,008 kilometers) through the heart of New Mexico. The Rio Grande then forms the southern boundary of Texas, separating the state from Mexico. At the end of its long journey, the Rio Grande empties into the Gulf of Mexico at Brownsville, Texas.

The Rio Grande is usually shallow. It is not suited for use as a major trade route. In all, the river drains about 172,000 square miles (447,200 square kilometers) of land. Most of this land is dry and barren, although dams and irrigation have made some areas farmable. *Tributaries* of the river, or smaller rivers that feed into it, include the Red, Chama, Santa Fe, and Pecos Rivers.

• Fast Fact •
Rio Grande **means "Great River" in Spanish.**
In Mexico, the river is called the *Río Bravo del Norte,*
or "Brave River of the North."

For about 1,300 miles (2,080 kilometers), the Rio Grande forms the international border between the United States and Mexico. The river has played a major role in U.S. and Mexican history. These two neighboring nations went to war over the river. As late as the 1960s, disputes over the river as an international boundary continued between the two countries.

Settlement

The first people to settle along the Rio Grande were the Pueblo (PWEB-loh) people. These early people built villages near the river. Their multistoried homes were made from *adobe* (uh-DOH-bee), or sun-baked clay. The Pueblos arrived in the area around 1000, migrating from the canyon regions to the north.

Some of the pueblo villages are still inhabited. One such ancient building is Taos (TAH-ohss) Pueblo. Located in Taos, New Mexico, the structure may have been built as early as A.D. 1000. About 150 members of the Taos tribe live in the pueblo today. Many more live nearby.

Other native tribes settled near the river. These tribes included the Jumano (joo-MAH-noh) and Tanpachoa (tan-PAH-choh-uh) in what is now west Texas, as well as the Coahuiltec (koh-uh-WEE-tek) and the Cotoname (koh-toh-NAH-mee) along the lower Rio Grande Valley.

Spanish Arrival

This portion of the Rio Grande near Cerro, New Mexico, is designated a National Wild and Scenic River area.

One of the first nonnatives to see the Rio Grande may have been Álvar Núñez Cabeza de Vaca (AHL-var NOON-yez kah-BAY-sah deh VAH-kah). A Spanish adventurer, Cabeza de Vaca was part of a 1528 expedition to Florida. The voyage was a disaster. On the return trip to Mexico, then called New Spain, Cabeza de Vaca and his crewmates were shipwrecked and stranded off the coast of Texas.

Over the next nine years, Cabeza de Vaca and three other survivors worked their way back to New Spain. Cabeza de Vaca eventually crossed the Rio Grande—the first European explorer to do so. Cabeza de Vaca returned to New Spain with tales of great cities filled with gold and other riches. These tales, told by the natives that Cabeza de Vaca had met, sparked further Spanish exploration to the Rio Grande area and beyond.

In 1540, Francisco Vásquez de Coronado (fran-SISS-koh VAHS-kez deh kor-oh-NAH-doh) set out to find the riches that Cabeza de Vaca had reported. In the spring of 1541, Coronado crossed the upper Rio Grande in what is now New Mexico. Although he did visit several pueblos during his journey, he did not discover gold and riches. Coronado continued his journey all the way to Kansas before returning to New Spain empty-handed and disappointed.

The first settlements in the Rio Grande area—and the Southwest—were founded by the Spanish beginning in the late 1500s. In 1598, Juan de Oñate (ohn-YAH-tay) led more than 400 settlers to the Rio Grande, which he formally claimed for Spain. He called the place where he crossed the river *el paso*, or "the ford." The settlement would later develop into the town of El Paso, Texas. Months later, Oñate arrived at San Juan Pueblo. He made San Juan the capital of *Nuevo Mexico*, or New Mexico.

The Spanish continued to found villages, missions, and forts, or *presidios*, along the Rio Grande. Many of the earliest Spanish settlements were in the region that is known today as New Mexico. Some early Spanish settlements in New Mexico that still exist today include Santa Fe, founded in 1610, and Albuquerque (AL-buh-ker-kee), founded in 1706.

One of the goals of the early Spanish settlers along the Rio Grande was to convert the native people to Christianity. The group built Catholic churches and missions throughout the region. They did not let natives practice their old religious (ree-LIH-jus) ways. They also forced some natives into slavery.

After enduring eighty years of Spanish rule, the Pueblo people had had enough. In the Pueblo Revolt of 1680, the Pueblo people rebelled against Spanish rule. United by a tribal leader named Popé, the Pueblos drove the Spanish out of the upper Rio Grande region.

This photograph from the 1860s shows the Ysleta tribe in front of the Church of San Antonio de Padua in the Pueblo Ysleta near El Paso, Texas.

During the Pueblo Revolt, the native warriors burned churches and other town buildings along the river. They also killed about 400 Spaniards, missionaries and settlers alike. The Pueblos captured Santa Fe and forced the Spanish to Ysleta (iz-LEH-tah), which is now part of El Paso. Ysleta was the first permanent settlement in Texas.

The Pueblo victory didn't last long. In 1689, Popé was murdered by his own people, and his once-successful alliance (uh-LYE-ense) fell apart. Just three years later, the Spanish were back. They easily defeated the Pueblos and began resettling the New Mexico region. By the early 1800s, about 30,000 Spanish colonists lived in the Rio Grande area.

One of the few non-Spanish adventurers in the Rio Grande area during this time was Réné-Robert Cavelier (kav-ul-YAY), sieur (lord) de La Salle. In 1684, La Salle founded a fort along the Gulf of Mexico in Matagorda Bay. Exploring the surrounding area, La Salle happened upon the mouth of the Rio Grande. He sailed upriver and may have built an outpost here. After La Salle was killed in 1687, the Spanish began sending more and more missionaries, soldiers, and settlers into the area. They wanted to make sure that the French did not trespass upon their territory. However, the biggest threat to the Spanish in the Southwest was yet to come.

American Arrival

One of the first Americans to explore the Rio Grande area was Zebulon Pike. In 1806, Pike began an expedition to explore the West for the U.S. Army. In February 1807, he was captured by the Spanish along the upper Rio Grande valley. Pike was jailed in Santa Fe and then taken to Chihuahua (chih-WAH-wuh), Mexico. Here, he was questioned by Spanish officials (uh-FISH-uls), who believed that he was a spy for the U.S. government.

Pike was finally released by the Spanish in June. Spanish officials escorted the explorer to the boundary of Spanish and American territory, and he was released in Louisiana. Pike managed to hide some of his diary and notes during his capture. He brought back news about the region, including trade opportunities along the river. Pike's reports sparked interest in the Southwest.

In 1821, Mexico won its independence (in-duh-PEN-dense) from Spain. The new Mexican government welcomed traders and limited settlement from the United States. Two years later, Americans began settling Texas. A man named Stephen Austin led the first group of 300 families into the area. Austin's father had received permission from the Spanish governors of New Spain to settle the land. Over the following years, Austin founded a number of settlements, bringing about 8,000 settlers into the region.

• *Fast Fact* •

Stephen Austin, who founded American settlements in Texas, is known as "the father of Texas."

As more and more settlers flooded into the Southwest, the Mexican government began having second thoughts. Soon, American settlers outnumbered Spanish and Mexican settlers in the region. The Mexicans decided that American migration into their territory must stop.

The Republic of Texas

In April 1830, Mexico's government banned new American settlers from entering their Southwestern territories. They also banned settlers from bringing slaves into the territory and imposed heavy taxes on American settlers living there. On October 2, 1835, the differences between the two groups came to a head in a battle near Gonzales, Texas. The battle marked the beginning of the Texas Revolution (1835–1836). Texas volunteers defeated Mexican troops at Gonzales and went on to win other battles, as well. By the end of 1835, they had forced Mexican troops back across the Rio Grande.

On March 2, 1836, a convention of Texans met to declare independence from Mexico. The Texans renamed their territory the Republic of Texas. Sam Houston (HYOO-stin) was named the first president of the republic. The Texas Revolution ended when Houston defeated Mexican dictator Antonio López de Santa Anna at the Battle of San Jacinto (hah-SIN-toh) in June 1836.

Texas was granted its independence from Mexico on the condition that it not become part of any other nation. However, interest in the region soon prompted many Americans to begin talking about *annexing*, or adding, Texas to the United States. There were plenty

The San Jacinto
Monument, a
570-foot obelisk,
marks the site of
the 1836 battle in
which the forces of
Texas defeated
Santa Anna's
army and won
independence
from Mexico.

of people who did not want to annex Texas. The
Republic of Texas had declared itself a slave-holding
territory. *Abolitionists*, people against slavery, did not
want to allow another slave state into the Union. For
nine years, the annexation arguments raged.

REMEMBER THE ALAMO

The most famous battle of the Texas Revolution (1835–1836) was the Battle of the Alamo. On February 23, 1836, Antonio López de Santa Anna led his troops into San Antonio. He attacked a group of American revolutionaries at the Alamo, a former Spanish mission. For twelve days, the Americans, fewer than 200 in number, managed to hold off more than 5,000 Mexican soldiers. On March 6, however, the Mexicans invaded the fort. They massacred all but two people there. Among the casualties were famed frontiersman Davy Crockett and James Bowie, inventor of the Bowie knife. For the rest of the Texas Revolution, "Remember the Alamo" was a rallying cry for Texans battling for independence (in-duh-PEN-dense).

The Mexican War

In 1845, John Tyler prepared to step down as president of the United States. Before he did, he signed a piece of paper that would start a war. Tyler put his signature on a bill to annex Texas. Mexico immediately broke off all relations with the United States.

Mexico also disputed the exact spot of the border between its land and Texas. The Republic of Texas had declared that the border between the two countries was the Rio Grande. Mexico disagreed. It said that the border was further north, along the Nueces (noo-AY-sess) River.

In January 1846, President James K. Polk decided to settle the dispute once and for all. He ordered General Zachary Taylor and 3,000 troops to advance from the Nueces River to the Rio Grande. At the site of what is now Brownsville, Texas, Taylor built a fort. The fort was opposite the Mexican town of Matamoros.

Mexican officials ordered Taylor to leave what they considered to be their territory. Taylor refused, and in April 1846, Mexican troops crossed the Rio Grande. The Mexicans attacked a patrol of American soldiers, killing or wounding sixteen.

That action was all that Polk needed. In May, he announced that Mexico had invaded U.S. territory. Congress declared war. The same month, Taylor and his men beat the Mexicans in the Battle of Resaca. The general continued his advance into Mexico from the north, while General Winfield Scott attacked from Mexico's east coast. Scott took Mexico's capital, Mexico City, in September 1847.

The war was officially over in February 1848 when both nations signed the Treaty of Guadalupe Hidalgo (gwahd-uh-LOOP hih-DAHL-goh). The treaty stated that the U.S.-Mexican border was the Rio Grande. In addition, the Mexicans ceded most of their remaining territory north of the river. This included California, Nevada, and Utah, as well as parts of Colorado, Arizona, New Mexico, and Wyoming. In all, Mexico gave up 500,000 square miles (1.3 million kilometers) of territory—nearly half of its entire area. In exchange, the United States paid Mexico $15 million and agreed to assume any financial claims by American citizens against Mexico.

The Battle of Resaca on May 9, 1846 is depicted in this drawing published by Nathaniel Currier in 1848.

This photo shows Abraham Lincoln as he looked in 1847.

AGAINST THE WAR

Not all Americans supported President James Polk's declaration of war against Mexico in 1846. One politician who strongly disagreed with the president was U.S. representative Abraham Lincoln. In Congress, Lincoln rose and attacked Polk's actions. Lincoln believed that the war was an excuse to add more slaveholding states to the Union.

Even after the war was over, border disputes between Mexico and the United States continued. In 1853, misunderstandings over the treaty led to the Gadsden Purchase. With the purchase, the United States bought nearly 30,000 square miles (78,000 square kilometers) of land. The land included parts of southern New Mexico and the southern section of Arizona.

New Americans

After the war, thousands of people who had considered themselves Mexican suddenly found themselves living in the United States. These people were given one year to decide whether they would remain in the Southwest and become Americans or return to Mexico. Only 2,000 chose to return; about 80,000 chose to stay.

Many Mexican-Americans found themselves the objects of discrimination and prejudice (PREH-joo-dis). Some had their land stolen from them by American settlers. Others found their land "legally" taken away by dishonest officials. The officials would often claim that the Mexican-Americans owed back taxes. Then the Mexican-Americans were forced to sell their land at just a fraction of what it was worth to pay these taxes.

In 1859, one man who had witnessed the discrimination decided to fight back. In September, Juan Cortina led a group of about eighty men into Brownsville. Cortina raised the Mexican flag over the city, and then he and his men went to work. Over the next few days, the men murdered four Americans that they believed were guilty of cheating Mexican-Americans. They also released all the Mexicans being held in Brownsville's jail. After a few days, Cortina left the town.

Many Mexicans saw Cortina as a freedom fighter, someone who was rebelling against American racism.

His cause was so popular that, at one point, he may have had as many as 600 men fighting with him. Some called him "the Robin Hood of the Rio Grande."

The Texas Rangers were sent to the Rio Grande to restore order. Founded in 1835, the rangers were a group of men on horseback who helped keep the peace in Texas. Over the next few months, skirmishes between Cortina and the rangers were common. However, the rangers were unable to stop Cortina. Finally, in February 1860, U.S. troops were sent to Texas. Cortina was forced to retreat, but he was never captured. During the Civil War (1861–1865), he returned to do battle with Confederate forces controlling Texas.

THE CIVIL WAR AND THE RIO GRANDE

Two months before the start of the Civil War (1861–1865), Texas broke away from the Union and joined the Confederate States of America. During the war, the Rio Grande became important to the Confederates. The Confederate army was able to get supplies from Mexico, a neutral country. For a time, Texas was also able to continue selling cotton to Mexico. This trade came to a halt, however, when Union troops took the lower river in 1863. That November, the Union army captured Brownsville, an important Confederate port. From Brownsville, Union troops were able to launch raids throughout the region.

Migration across the Rio Grande

To many Mexicans, the Rio Grande represents the last barrier to a better life in the United States. In 1910, the first big wave of Mexicans crossed the river into Texas to escape the Mexican Revolution (1910–1920). Riverside towns grew rapidly, their numbers swelled by the newcomers.

In 1924, the United States set up a border patrol along the Rio Grande. U.S. officials wanted to make sure that Mexicans crossing into Texas were doing so legally. That meant that each person crossing the river needed permission. Over the years, high fences have been built along the river. The number of border patrol agents has increased, too.

Today, Mexicans continue trying to cross the Rio Grande into the United States. In 2000, about 1 million Mexicans were caught trying to enter the United States illegally. Mexicans who are caught crossing the border illegally are returned to Mexico. Once there, they often try again. It is estimated that more than 200,000 illegal immigrants make it into the United States from Mexico each year.

The trip into the United States can be costly. Some Mexicans pay *coyotes* (kye-OH-teez), guides who make a living by taking groups of people across the border. The one-way trip can cost hundreds of dollars. The journey across the river can also be very dangerous. Additionally, some coyotes are dishonest. They may abandon their customers at the first sign of trouble. Some groups of would-be immigrants have been left locked in car trunks and vans in sweltering desert heat by coyotes.

Between 1993 and 1996, more than 1,000 immigrants died trying to reach the United States from Mexico. In the year 2000 alone, the number of deaths related to this border crossing was more than 380. Some die as a result of coyotes' actions. Many drown in the Rio Grande. Others are hit by vehicles (VEE-ik-ulz) while trying to cross highways and roads.

• Fast Fact •

In 2000, an organization called American Rivers named the Rio Grande one of the most endangered rivers in the United States.

Commerce

Ranching, farming, and manufacturing are important industries along the Rio Grande. Mining, begun in the late sixteenth century, also contributes to the region's economy. Petroleum, gas, coal, silver, gypsum, and potash have all been taken from the lower river area.

Ranching and Farming

Most of the land along the Rio Grande is very dry. Before irrigation was available, the land was not suitable for large-scale farming. The grassy areas along the riverbanks were, however, great for grazing livestock. As a result, one of the chief industries in the early days of settlement was ranching.

opposite:
Cowboys herd
cattle into a pen
near Goliad,
Texas as part of
the city's 250th
anniversary as the
birthplace of
Texas ranching.

Cattle ranching has been important to the Rio Grande region since the first Spanish settlers came to the area. The first cowboys were Spaniards and Native Americans who were trained by missionaries to ride horses and herd cattle. These men were known as *vaqueros* (vah-KAYR-ose). Later, American ranchers would borrow many of the words and practices of the vaqueros.

In the late 1800s, sheep were also grazed along the river in large numbers. The wool from these animals was sent down the river. From Brownsville, it was then shipped to the Northeastern textile factories. Sheep ranching peaked in the 1880s. By 1910, the grassy plains had been overgrazed, and the trade was not as important as it once was.

Cattle and sheep ranching both continue in the region today. Farming, too, has become an important part of the region's economy. Thanks to irrigation projects along the river in Texas and New Mexico, cash crops are now able to be grown here. These crops include citrus fruits, vegetables, and cotton.

WORKING WORDS

Many of the words we associate with cowboys and ranching come from the early Spanish *vaqueros* (vah-KAYR-ose), or cowboys.

Cowboy Word	Spanish Word	Meaning
bronco	bronco	rough, wild
buckaroo	vaquero	cowboy
lariat	la reata	the rope
lasso	lazo	noose
mustang	mestengo	stray
ranch	rancho	small ranch
rodeo	rodear	surround
stampede	estampida	crash

Manufacturing

Manufacturing is a very important part of the Rio Grande's economy. *Maquiladoras* (mah-kil-ah-DOR-ahs), also known as "twin plants," operate along the U.S.-Mexican border. The maquiladoras are factories where pieces of U.S. and foreign goods are sent to be put together. The cost of labor at the maquiladoras is much lower than in U.S. plants. This means that goods can be produced for less money. It also means that maquiladora workers are paid much less than workers in the United States.

Most of the maquiladoras are owned by U.S. companies. They assemble U.S. car parts, electronics, plastics, and clothing. The factories have been an important part of the regional economy since the 1980s. They have also served to boost the populations of border towns on both sides of the Rio Grande.

Tourism

Tourism is another important industry along the Rio Grande. People from around the world come to experience (ex-PEER-ee-ense) the unique (yoo-NEEK) blend of Spanish, Native American, and American cultures that exists nowhere else. The warm climate, complete with sunshine and low humidity, also attracts visitors to the region.

Albuquerque is a popular vacation destination in New Mexico. The city became well known in the early 1900s as a place where people with the disease tuberculosis could come to feel better. Today, the city is better known for its International Balloon Festival. During the ten-day festival, hundreds of hot-air balloons take to the sky.

Along the Rio Grande in Texas, there is much to see and do. People from both sides of the border enjoy the Amistad National Recreation Area in Del Rio, Texas. The recreation area, which includes a large

*opposite:
About 600 hot air balloons fly over Albuquerque, New Mexico as part of the International Balloon Fiesta.*

reservoir (REH-zerv-wahr) for fishing, swimming, and boating, spans the Rio Grande. Amistad is shared by both the United States and Mexico. Big Bend National Park is another popular attraction.

Towns along the river also attract visitors. El Paso, Rio Grande City, Brownsville, and other historic towns offer a unique cultural experience to visitors. These three cities are also ports of entry between Mexico and the United States. With the proper paperwork, Americans can cross into another country—Mexico—here.

Today

As the Rio Grande area has become more populated, the river itself has suffered. Water pollution has increased dramatically over the years. Runoff pesticides (PESS-tih-sydez) and fertilizers from local farms, as well as chemicals (KEM-ik-ulz) and even untreated sewage, have found their way into the water. The water is not safe to swim in or drink.

In recent years, Mexico and the United States have been working together to clean up the Rio Grande. In 1992, the two nations issued a plan of action to study the problem. They promised to cooperate to reduce river pollution.

Riverside cities and conservation groups have also pitched in to end pollution. In El Paso, for example, city officials are working hard to educate residents about their river. In 2000, they began a campaign to stem dumping in the river. Groups like the Rio Grande/Rio Bravo Basin Coalition have formed to raise awareness about the pollution problem, too.

TRUTH OR CONSEQUENCES

In 1950, people living in Hot Springs, New Mexico, decided it was time for a change. They renamed their town Truth or Consequences after a popular radio game show, *Truth or Consequences*.

Rocky Mountains

6

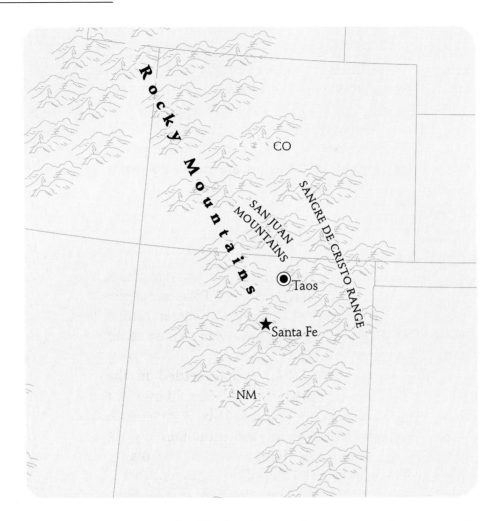

The Rocky Mountains are a major mountain system that stretches about 3,000 miles (4,800 kilometers) across the North American continent. The Rockies begin in Alaska and extend down through Canada and into the West, ending in central New Mexico in the Southwest region. Called the continent's backbone or spine, the Rockies are the largest mountain system in North America.

The Rockies run in a long, fairly straight line that is 350 miles (560 kilometers) wide in some areas. In the Southwest, the Sangre de Cristo and San Juan ranges make up the Rocky Mountains. Several important cities are located in the foothills of the two ranges, including Taos (TAH-ohss) and Santa Fe, New Mexico. Santa Fe is the capital of New Mexico.

The Rockies are an area that is rich in mineral and other natural resources. With its high peaks, magnificent (mag-NIH-fih-sent) wildlife, and other majestic scenes, the region is also one of breathtaking beauty. As a result, the Rockies are home to many national parks and forests.

Settlement

Some of the earliest arrivals in the Rocky Mountains of the Southwest may have been the Folsom people. These early ancestors (AN-sess-terz) of later Native American tribes arrived in the New Mexico area about 10,000 years ago.

Later, Pueblo (PWEB-loh) people settled in the area. Their villages, called *pueblos*, were known for their multistoried adobe (uh-DOH-bee) dwellings. *Adobe* is sun-baked clay. In the mountain region, villages included Taos, Jemez, and Pena Blanca Pueblos in New Mexico. Some Pueblo groups crossed the Sangre de Cristo Mountains to hunt bison on the Great Plains.

THE PECOS RIVER

The Pecos River, an important river in the Southwest, has its source in the Sangre de Cristo Mountains. The river flows 926 miles (1,482 kilometers) through New Mexico and Texas before emptying into the Rio Grande. The Carlsbad Caverns are located near the river in Carlsbad, New Mexico. The caverns make up one of the largest underground cave systems in the world.

HIGH PEAKS OF THE SOUTHWESTERN ROCKIES

Range	Peak	State	Elevation
Sangre de Cristo	Blanca Peak	Colorado	14,345 feet (4,304 meters)
Sangre de Cristo	Wheeler Peak	New Mexico	13,161 feet (3,948 meters)
Sangre de Cristo	Truchas Peak	New Mexico	13,102 feet (3,931 meters)
San Juan	Uncompahgre Peak	Colorado	14,309 feet (4,293 meters)
San Juan	Mount Sneffels	Colorado	14,150 feet (4,245 meters)
San Juan	Santa Clara Peak	New Mexico	11,562 feet (3,469 meters)

The Pueblos were living in the area when Europeans began exploring there. One of the first outsiders to encounter the Pueblos was Spanish explorer Francisco Vásquez de Coronado (fran-SISS-koh VAHS-kez deh kor-oh-NAH-doh). Coronado entered the Sangre de Cristo region in 1540, exploring as far north as Taos. The Spanish *conquistador* (kohn-KEESS-tah-dor), or conqueror, searching for gold and other treasures, was disappointed in the region. He returned to New Spain (Mexico) convinced that the area was useless.

In 1598, the Spanish began settling New Mexico. That year, Juan de Oñate (ohn-YAH-tay) named San Juan Pueblo, a few miles north of Santa Fe, as the capital of the New Mexico Territory. In 1609, Don Pedro de Peralta became governor-general of the region. He moved the territorial capital to Santa Fe.

The first European roadway in the United States was created by the Spanish to reach Santa Fe. El Camino

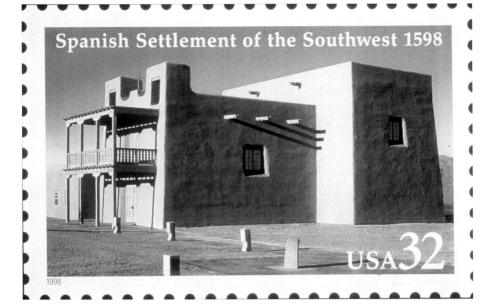

Spanish Settlement of the Southwest 1598

USA32

1998

Real de Tierra Adentro (the Royal Road of the Interior Lands) stretched for 1,800 miles (2,880 kilometers) from Mexico City into Spain's northern territories. The roadway followed the Rio Grande into New Mexico, through Belen and Albuquerque (AL-buh-ker-kee), before ending in Santa Fe.

This stamp issued by the U.S. Postal Service commemorates the 400th anniversary of El Camino Real de Tierra Adentro, the oldest European road in the United States.

As capital of the region, Santa Fe served as the headquarters for the surrounding Spanish missions and settlements. Missions sprang up in the area to convert the native peoples to Christianity. The Pueblos, however, did not want to be converted. In 1680, they attacked Santa Fe. They killed 400 settlers and burned most of the town's buildings to the ground. The Spanish were forced to retreat from the region.

The Pueblos enjoyed twelve years of peace. Then in 1692, the Spanish returned and took Santa Fe. Within a few years, they had regained control of the entire region. During the Spanish era, a number of adventurers attempted to explore and map the Rocky Mountain region. From 1761 to 1765, Juan de Rivera explored much of the San Juan Mountains, searching for gold. Like Coronado, he returned home disappointed.

A decade later, Silvestre Vélez de Escalante (sil-VESS-tray VELL-ehz deh es-kahl-AHN-tay) and Francisco Atanasio Dominguez (fran-SISS-koh ah-tah-NAHS-ee-oh doh-MING-ez) charted a path through the mountains. The two missionaries were searching for a route from Santa Fe to Spanish missions on the California coast. They wanted to find a route that bypassed the deserts of the Southwest and West. The two men reached what is now Utah before turning back. Their course would become the southern section of a trail to Los Angeles (los AN-jell-ess), California, known as the Old Spanish Trail.

American Arrival

For more than 125 years, the Spanish dominated the New Mexico area. Spain discouraged outsiders from venturing into the region. In 1807, Zebulon Pike crossed the Rocky Mountains from Colorado into New Mexico. Pike was arrested by Spanish officials (uh-FISH-uls) and imprisoned in Santa Fe. He was later sent to a prison in Mexico before being kicked out of Spanish lands.

In 1821, Mexico gained its independence (in-duh-PEN-dense) from Spain. American traders and travelers found that the Mexican government was much more welcoming than the Spanish one had been. One of the first Americans to take advantage of the new air of hospitality was trader William Becknell, who visited Santa Fe in 1821.

Eventually, the United States and Mexico went to war over control of the Southwest. In August 1846, three months after the start of the Mexican War (1846–1848), U.S. general Stephen Watts Kearny took control of Santa Fe. Kearny raised the American flag over the city's plaza, and from that moment onward, the Rocky Mountain region of the Southwest was under American control. The only time it fell out of U.S. hands was in 1863, when Santa Fe was held briefly by Confederate troops during the Civil War (1861–1865).

opposite:
This painting shows Stephen Watts Kearny, the general who conquered New Mexico, in his military uniform.

After the war, the Americans took control, and a number of groups explored the Rocky Mountain regions. In 1848, John C. Frémont took a party of men through the San Juan Mountains. Frémont hoped to find another route to California. Despite his reputation as "the Great Pathfinder," Frémont's journey was a disaster. Half his party died; the rest made their way to Taos.

Commerce

This lithograph shows a settlement on the Santa Fe Trail.

After 1821, American merchants began traveling into the New Mexico Territory. They brought goods with them from around the United States to trade. The first American trader to arrive in Santa Fe was William Becknell in 1821. The following year, Becknell was back with wagonloads of goods to sell in the Southwest.

• Fast Fact •
**Santa Fe, New Mexico,
founded in 1610,
is the oldest state capital
in the United States.**

Becknell was the first person to open up a pathway from the Midwest to the Southwest. The route, which began in Independence, Missouri, was known as the Santa Fe Trail. The trail, more than 780 miles (1,248 kilometers) long, completely avoided crossing the Sangre de Cristo range. Instead, wagon trains traveled around the bottom of the mountains to the south before heading back north to Santa Fe.

ARTISTS AND AUTHORS IN NEW MEXICO

Lew Wallace: From 1878 to 1881, Wallace served as governor of the New Mexico Territory. In 1880, he also found the time to publish the novel *Ben Hur.* Several movies were later made of the book.

Georgia O'Keeffe: O'Keeffe was an artist who first visited New Mexico in 1929. Her paintings of desert flowers and landscapes became world famous. O'Keeffe moved to New Mexico in 1949 and lived there until her death in 1986.

D.H. Lawrence: In the 1920s, Lawrence, a famed British writer, spent eleven months at a ranch near Taos (TAH-ohss). Lawrence later called his time in New Mexico his "greatest experience [ex-PEER-ee-ense] from the outside world."

The Santa Fe Trail was the busiest and most important trail into the Southwest. Each year, thousands of wagons traveled over the route. As the last stop on the trail, Santa Fe became an important market city. Here, trappers and traders sold animal pelts and other wares. Taos was another important trading center. During the war with Mexico, the trail was a major route for military troops and supplies into the Southwest.

In 1870, construction of the Atchison, Topeka, and Santa Fe Railroad began. When completed, the railway stretched from Atchison, Kansas, across Colorado and New Mexico, and finally, it looped into Texas. An important stop along the line was Santa Fe. The railway followed parts of the Santa Fe Trail. In some places, the railway tracks were laid out over old wagon ruts in the trail. The Santa Fe Trail was a major trade route between Santa Fe and the Midwest.

In 1878, the railroad company dug a tunnel 2,000 feet (600 meters) long through the Sangre de Cristo Mountains, from Colorado into New Mexico. In 1880, the Atchison, Topeka, and Santa Fe Railroad steamed into Santa Fe for the first time. The golden days of the Santa Fe Trail were over.

opposite:
Visitors explore
Indian ruins
in Bandelier
National Park
near Los Alamos,
New Mexico.

Today

Tourism is an important part of the Rocky Mountain economy in the Southwest. Visitors have been coming to the region since the early 1900s. After New Mexico gained its statehood in 1912, Santa Fe attracted attention as a healing place. The area's warm, dry climate was believed to be the perfect cure for tuberculosis, an infection of the lungs.

Today, the region is known for its unique (yoo-NEEK) blend of Native American, Spanish, and American cultures. Santa Fe, for example, is a popular destination for vacationers. Visitors can enjoy the

Museum of Indian Arts and Culture, the Georgia O'Keeffe Museum, and the Palace of the Governors. Built in 1610, the palace is the oldest public building in the United States.

Winter sports and hiking are also popular pastimes in the mountains. Taos is a hot spot for skiers. Hikers can trek through several national parklands in the area. These parklands include Aztec Ruins, Bandelier, and Chaco Canyon National Monuments. Vacationers can visit the ruins of ancient pueblos and cliff dwellings in the parks.

Sonoran Desert

7

The Sonoran Desert is a vast, arid region that covers more than 100,000 square miles (260,000 square kilometers) in Arizona, California, and Mexico. In the Southwest, the Sonoran Desert covers most of southwestern Arizona. The Sonoran Desert is one of the hottest, driest regions in North America. During the long, hot summer months, temperatures regularly climb up to 100°F (38°C). Like all other deserts, the region receives little rainfall.

The Sonoran Desert is known as a "green desert" for its wealth of plant life. Plants in the Sonoran Desert include many different kinds of cacti. One unique (yoo-NEEK) cactus, found nowhere else on Earth, is the saguaro (sah-GWAR-oh) cactus. Saguaro cacti can grow to be 50 feet (15 meters) tall and 10 tons (9 metric tons) in weight. They may live for 200 years. Other desert plants include ironwood and Joshua trees as well as creosote (KREE-uh-soht) and sage bushes.

Although the Sonoran Desert region is generally low-lying and flat, there are several mountain ranges within the desert's borders. In Arizona, these ranges include the Chocolate, Kofa, and Harquahala (har-kwuh-HAH-lah) Mountains. A number of rivers also flow through the desert, including the Colorado, Gila, and Salt Rivers.

Settlement

The first people to make their homes in the Sonoran Desert may have arrived there as early as 10,000 years ago. By A.D. 300, the Hohokam (ho-HO-kum) people thrived near what is now Phoenix (FEE-nix). Some historians believe that the Hohokam may have migrated north from what is now Mexico. These early people built canal systems from the Salt and Gila Rivers to irrigate their crops. They grew corn, beans, squash, cotton, and other items.

• Fast Fact •

The name *Hohokam* comes from a Pima (PEEM-uh) word meaning "all gone" or "all used up." The Pima used the word to describe the early peoples—who had disappeared—to the Spanish.

Around 1300, the Hohokam constructed a large, four-story mud building near what is now Coolidge, Arizona. Spanish explorers who came across the building dubbed it *Casa Grande*, or "Great House." The remains of Casa Grande still stand in the desert. The Hohokam people disappeared from the Sonoran region in the mid-1400s. Some historians believe that they may have left to escape a drought.

Later tribes in the area included the Yaqui (YAH-kee), Yuma (YOO-muh), Tohono O'odham (toh-HOH-noh AH-ah-tum), and Pima (PEEM-uh). The Pima may have been the descendants (dee-SEN-dentz) of the earlier Hohokam people. Like the Hohokam, the Pima also built canals to irrigate their crops.

Spanish Settlement

The first European explorers in the Sonoran Desert were Spaniards who arrived in the 1500s. One of the first to cross the arid region was Melchior (MEL-kee-ohr) Diaz in 1540. Diaz was part of the expedition led by Francisco Vásquez de Coronado (fran-SISS-koh VAHS-kez deh kor-oh-NAH-doh) through the Southwest. The expedition was looking for gold and treasure. Coronado sent Diaz and a group of men to the Gulf of California to meet supply ships.

Diaz made his way through the Sonoran region, crossing the Colorado River near what is now Yuma, Arizona. Diaz missed the supply ships, however, and he and his men turned around to begin the long trip back. During the return trip, Diaz died and was buried somewhere in the desert.

In 1595, explorer Juan de Oñate (ohn-YAH-tay) claimed the Southwest, including the Sonoran Desert area, for Spain. Although Spain founded missions and presidios, or forts, in other parts of the Southwest, the Sonoran Desert was ignored for nearly 100 years. Then in 1692, Eusebio Francisco Kino (ay-yoo-SAY-bee-oh fran-SISS-koh KEE-noh) arrived in the region.

• Fast Fact •

In addition to being a missionary and an explorer, Father Eusebio Francisco Kino (ay-yoo-SAY-bee-oh fran-SISS-koh KEE-noh) was also a mapmaker. His drawings of the region, including a map of Baja California, were used for many years after his death.

A DIVERSE DESERT

The Sonoran Desert has the most diverse plant and animal life of any North American desert. Scientists estimate that there are about 2,000 species (SPEE-sheez) of plants; 550 species of reptiles, birds, and mammals; and an unknown number of insects. Wild desert animals include the elf owl; Gila monster; sidewinder; desert tortoise; western diamondback; turkey vulture; peccary; kangaroo rat; coyote (kye-OH-tee); bobcat; tarantula; scorpion; and roadrunner.

Golden poppies fill a field in Organ Pipe Cactus Monument in the Sonoran Desert of southern Arizona.

Kino was an Italian explorer and Jesuit missionary working for Spain. Kino's goal was to convert the Native American tribes in the region to Christianity.

Kino remained in the Sonoran region until his death in 1711. During his time there, Kino founded at least twenty-four missions in Arizona and California. One of Kino's missions in the Sonoran Desert was San Xavier del Bac, near what is now Tucson (TOO-sahn), Arizona. Kino taught the natives new ways of farming and introduced cattle and sheep to the area.

Although Father Kino was kind to the native peoples, the majority of Spanish settlers who came to the region were not. After Kino's death, hatred for the Spanish grew among some area tribes. In 1781, a group of Yuma people wiped out two Spanish settlements near the Gila and Colorado Rivers. The Spanish did not rebuild these settlements.

opposite: Grand rock formations line the walls of many caverns in Colossal Cave Mountain Park near Tucson, Arizona.

COLOSSAL CAVE

Located near Tucson (TOO-sahn), Arizona, Colossal Cave is a cave that was used by the Hohokam people as a storage space and shrine. Rediscovered in 1879 by area residents, the cave was later used as a hideout for prison escapees and train robbers. Some of the earliest tours through the cave took place in 1923. Visitors were tied together with rope and guided through the cave by lamplight. The cave's amazing features include strange and wonderful rock formations, such as Kingdom of the Elves and the Silent Waterfall. Another such formation is the Crystal Forest, a group of stalactites that drip from the ceiling of one of the cave's many rooms. Today, the cave is part of Colossal Cave Mountain Park.

American Arrival

Americans began exploring and settling the Sonoran Desert in 1821, after Mexico became independent from Spain. American trappers, traders, and travelers began venturing into the Southwest, including the Sonoran Desert region. For most early travelers, the desert was a place to hurry through on their way to other destinations.

One trail through the desert was the Gila Trail. The trail stretched through New Mexico and Arizona before ending near Los Angeles (los AN-jell-ess), California. It was used first by the Spanish, but later by American hunters and traders. During the California gold rush, the Gila Trail became one of the chief paths through the desert to the gold fields of California. The city of Yuma had its start as a supply stop for miners on their way there.

In the late 1840s, the United States fought the Mexican War (1846–1848) with Mexico over control of the Southwest. After the United States defeated Mexico, the two nations signed the Treaty of Guadalupe Hidalgo (gwahd-uh-LOOP hih-DAHL-goh). According to the treaty, the United States gained the land north of the Gila River.

In 1853, the United States bought a 30,000-square-mile (78,000-square-kilometer) strip of land along the U.S.-Mexico border. The purchase included the Sonoran Desert region of Arizona, as well as part of New Mexico. The sale became known as the Gadsden Purchase, named after diplomat James Gadsden, who negotiated the sale with Mexico.

Phoenix, the settlement that would eventually become Arizona's largest city, got its start in 1867. By 1880, Phoenix was a booming frontier town, with more than 2,400 residents. The town had its own telegraph line, an ice factory, a newspaper, sixteen saloons, and four dance halls.

Settlement in the region was boosted by the arrival of the Southern Pacific (puh-SIFF-ik) Railroad. In 1877, the railroad arrived in Yuma; three years later, it puffed into Tucson. In 1887, the rail lines to Phoenix were completed. Settlers now found it easier to get into the desert, and they began coming in ever-larger numbers.

After World War II (1939–1945), the desert became a popular place to settle down. Many veterans relocated to the warm, dry region. The cities of Phoenix and Tucson flourished, and other towns sprang up nearby. In later years, senior citizens were also attracted by the sunny climate. In 1960, a large senior community called Sun City was built near Phoenix. Sun City is the largest retirement community in the nation. No one under the age of eighteen is allowed to live there.

Today, 80 percent of Arizona's population lives in the Sonoran Desert region. The largest metropolitan areas in the state are here, including Tucson, Yuma, Tempe (TEMP-ee), Scottsdale, and Phoenix. Phoenix, on the eastern edge of the desert, is the state's capital.

A number of Native American reservations are also located in the Sonoran Desert region. They include the Salt River (Pima and Maricopa), Gila River (Akimel O'odham), Papago Indian (Tohono O'odham), and Cocopah (Yuma) Reservations. About 19,000 Native Americans live on the reservations.

WHAT'S IN A NAME?

Phoenix (FEE-nix), Arizona, was named after a mythical bird that is destroyed by fire yet rises, whole, from its own ashes.

Tucson was originally called *Stook-zone*, a native word meaning "water at the foot of black mountain."

Yuma (YOO-muh) is named for the Yuma tribe that lived in the area. Before it was called Yuma, however, the town was known as Colorado City and Arizona City at different times.

Commerce

Believe it or not, agriculture is one of the most important industries in the Sonoran Desert region. Today, the desert is one of the largest irrigated areas in the Southwest. Development of the area for farming began in 1867, when Jack Swilling arrived in Phoenix. Swilling saw the ancient canals that the Hohokam people had built there. Shortly after arriving, he founded a canal company. He began to rebuild the canals in the area that the Hohokam people had constructed more than 400 years before. Swilling irrigated the surrounding area and made it a fertile farming region. By 1886, there were about 240 miles (384 kilometers) of canals in the Phoenix area. Wheat and figs were among the earliest crops.

Crops grown in the Sonoran region today include cotton, vegetables, fruits, wheat, alfalfa, and barley. Cattle ranching, which began in the 1880s, is also important to the local economy.

JOJOBA

Jojoba (hoh-HOH-buh), a shrub that grows wild in the Sonoran Desert, may someday be an important desert crop. The seeds of the jojoba contain a great deal of oil. The oil, which doesn't become *rancid*, or rotten, is currently used to make shampoos, cosmetics, and other items. Some scientists believe that jojoba oil could be used as an industrial lubricant or machine oil. Someday, jojoba might even replace vegetable oil! A number of jojoba plantations have been established in the Sonoran Desert.

Getting Water
from the Desert

Ever since people first settled and worked in the Sonoran Desert region, their greatest challenge has been finding a good supply of water. The amount of rainfall that the desert receives each year has never been enough to meet

the area's needs. Most of the area's drinking water comes from underground or nearby rivers, including the Colorado, Gila, and Salt Rivers.

The first large-scale efforts at water control in the Sonoran Desert began in 1905 on the Salt River. Dams were built on the river to control floods and provide enough water for farming and drinking. The first dam built on the Salt was the Roosevelt Dam, completed in 1911.

The Salt River created a good water supply for metropolitan Arizona in the early 1900s. As the area became more popular, however, city leaders realized that a new source of water was needed. In 1963, the U.S. Supreme Court ruled that Arizona had water rights to the Colorado River. After more than a decade of construction, the Central Arizona Project (CAP) was completed in 1985. Today, CAP delivers millions of gallons of water from the Colorado River each day to meet the needs of the region. Three out of every four Arizonans receive water or power from CAP through a network of canals, pipelines, and tunnels.

> **• Fast Fact •**
> **The Roosevelt Dam was named after Theodore Roosevelt, who had initiated the water-control project during his U.S. presidency.**

Other Area Industries

Several other industries help keep the Sonoran Desert economy healthy. Mining, for example, has been carried out in the desert since the mid-1850s. In 1858, miners took gold from the Gila and lower Colorado Rivers. Other minerals taken from the area include copper, silver, and lead.

The U.S. military has a strong presence in the Sonoran region. During World War II, military bases, landing sites, and firing ranges were built in the desert. Bases in the region include Luke Air Force Base, near Phoenix, and Davis-Monthan Air Force Base, near Tucson. Thousands of U.S. troops have been trained in the Sonoran Desert.

In recent decades, people looking for places to locate their businesses began choosing the Sonoran Desert. The area's warm, dry climate and beautiful scenery

(SEEN-er-ee) are among the factors that attract new manufacturing businesses. Sports equipment, electronics, processed foods, clothing, and many other items are made in area factories.

Tourism

Tourism is important in the Sonoran Desert. Since the early 1900s, tourists have come to the area to enjoy the year-round sunshine, warm temperatures, and low humidity. Today, tourists can visit the many thriving cities in the region, including Phoenix, Tucson, and Yuma. The Sonoran Desert also has a wealth of national parklands.

Saguaro National Park covers more than 91,000 acres (36,400 hectares) of land. Visitors to this national park can see saguaro cacti, Gila monsters, and other desert dwellers. Saguaro was made a national park in 1994.

Joshua Tree National Park covers nearly 560,000 acres (224,000 hectares) of land. It was designated a national park in 1994 to preserve the rare Joshua trees that grow within its limits.

Organ Pipe Cactus National Monument has more than 330,000 acres (132,000 hectares) of wild desert land. Established in 1937, the area includes the Camino del Diablo Trail, a pathway from Mexico to the gold fields of California.

Imperial National Wildlife Refuge and Kofa National Wildlife Refuge are located near Yuma. These areas have been set aside as a refuge for wild birds and other animals.

• Fast Fact •

The saguaro (sah-GWAR-oh) cactus flower is Arizona's state flower.

DESERT SPORTS

The Sonoran region is home to several professional sports teams.

• *Phoenix Suns*—This National Basketball Association team got its start in 1968. Team players have included Charles Barkley, Kevin Johnson, and Alvan Adams.

• *Arizona Cardinals*—This National Football League team moved from St. Louis, Missouri, to Tempe (TEMP-ee), Arizona, in 1988. Founded in 1898, the Cardinals are the oldest continuously run NFL team still playing.

• *Phoenix Coyotes* (kye-OH-teez)—Once known as the Winnipeg Jets, this National Hockey League team began playing in Phoenix in 1996.

• *Arizona Diamondbacks*—The Diamondbacks, a Major League Baseball team, began playing in Phoenix in 1998. In 2001, the team won the World Series.

Today

People love to visit the Sonoran Desert, and many decide to stay. Over the years, Phoenix has grown. Its borders are constantly expanding into the desert. Suburbs around the region's other large cities are also constantly growing.

Some people have begun to worry that the desert environment will be ruined by all this new development, known as *urban sprawl*. More people in the region means more pollution. Air pollution can kill plants in the desert and harm animals that live there.

opposite: Frank Lloyd Wright designed his winter home, Taliesin West, in Arizona's Sonoran Desert to complement the environment with sharp angles and sloping roofs.

More people in the region also means a greater demand for water. As a result, water conservation is a constant concern in the desert. Beginning in 1980, strict water conservation laws were passed in Arizona. Residents must be extra careful to use this precious resource wisely.

BIOSPHERE II

In 1991, a group of *ecologists*, people who study the environment, entered a big, dome-shaped building built in the middle of the Sonoran Desert. For the next two years, they lived sealed up inside the building, called Biosphere (BYE-ohs-feer) II (the planet Earth is Biosphere I). They grew their own food and tried to live without any outside help. The ecologists hoped to prove that people might someday live inside such an environment in space. Unfortunately, the experiment was not completely successful. After sixteen months inside, oxygen levels dropped to dangerously low levels, and fresh air had to be pumped into the building.

Although the experiment didn't quite succeed as planned, Biosphere II is still used. Today, the building is owned by Columbia University, and research is conducted there.

Sources

BOOKS

Ansary, Mir Tamin. *Southwest Indians.* Des Plaines, IL: Heinemann Library, 2000.

Dary, David. *The Santa Fe Trail: Its History, Legends, and Lore.* New York: A. A. Knopf, 2000.

Frazier, Ian. *On the Rez.* New York: Farrar, Straus, and Giroux, 2000.

Hesse, Karen. *Out of the Dust.* New York: Scholastic, 1997.

Hoyt-Goldsmith, Diane. *Migrant Worker: A Boy from the Rio Grande Valley.* New York: Holiday House, 1996.

Maurer, Richard. *The Wild Colorado.* New York: Crown Publishers, 1999.

Meltzer, Milton. *Driven from the Land: The Story of the Dust Bowl.* Tarrytown, NY: Benchmark Books, 2000.

Rasmussen, R. Kent. *Pueblo.* Vero Beach, FL: Rourke Book Company, 2001.

Stein, R. Conrad. *In the Spanish West.* Tarrytown, NY: Benchmark Books, 2000.

WEB SITES

Arizona-Sonora Desert Museum *www.desertmuseum.org/*

Borderlands Information Center *www.riogrande.org/*

The Handbook of Texas Online
 www.tsha.utexas.edu/handbook/online/index.new.html

National Park Service—Grand Canyon National Park
 www.nps.gov/grca/index.htm

The On-line Sonoran Desert Educational Center
 www.co.pima.az.us/cmo/sdcp/sdcp2/edu/

Texas Beyond History—Red River War
 www.texasbeyondhistory.net/redriver/index.html

The Tornado Project Online *www.tornadoproject.com/*

Index

abolitionists 87
Adams-Onís Treaty 68
Adams, John Quincy 68
adobe *ix*, 81
Alamo 88
Alarcón, Hernando de 5–6
Alaska 100
All-American Canal 15
Allen, Augustus and John 51
America vii, 7, 18, 26, 37, 47, 48, 49, 64,
  68, 70, 75, 85, 86, 88, 94, 96, 100, 106,
  109, 112, 118
Amistad National Recreation Area 96, 98
animals 115, 123
Antelope Canyon xi
archaeologists 77
Arizona vii, viii, x, 2, 3, 15, 17, 89, 91,
  112, 113, 115, 118, 122, 124
  Bullhead City 11
  Coolidge 113
  La Paz County 5
  Phoenix vii, 16, 118, 119, *121*
  Scottsdale 119
  Tucson 117, 119
Arkansas 38, 62, 63, 77
Army Corps of Engineers 78
artists 107
Atchison, Topeka, and
  Santa Fe Railroad 109
Atlantic Ocean 44
Austin, Stephen 85, 86
authors 107
Aztec Ruins 110

Bandelier National Park *109*, 110
barrier islands 46
Battle of Resaca *89*
Battle of San Jacinto *50*
Becknell, William 104, 106–107
Bering Sea 45
Big Bend National Park 98
Biosphere II 126
Black Canyon 7, 15
Bowie, James 88

Cabeza de Vaca, Álvar Nuñez 46, *47*,
  82–83
California 2, 3, 7, 10, 15, 37, 38, 68, 89,
  104, 112, 123
  Baja 114
  Bakersville 37
  Los Angeles 16, 104, 118
  San Bernardino County 5

Camino del Diablo Trail 123
camps 38
Canada 20, 100
Canadian River 24
canoes 45, 75
Cardeñas, Garcia Lopez de 5
Caribbean Sea 44
Casa Grande 113
cattle drives 32, 33, 68, 76, 77
Central Arizona Project (CAP) 122
Chaco Canyon *4*, 10
Chama River 84
Chisholm Trail 33, 76
Chocolate Mountains 113
Civil War 7, *8*, 35, 48, 49, 51, *69*, 92, 104
cliffs 3, 4
climate vii, ix, 11, 44, 112, 122
Colorado 2, 36, 80, 89
  Denver 33
Colorado River 2–7, 9–10, 11, 12–13,
  15–16, 114, 117, 121, 122
Colossal Cave Mountain Park *116*, 117
continental shelf 57
Coronado, Francisco Vázquez de viii, 5,
  6, 22–23, 64, 83, 102, 103, 114
corporations 34, 55, 96
Cortina, Juan 91–92
cowboys 32–33, 76, 94, *95*
coyotes 93
Crockett, Davy 88
crop rotation 38
Cuba 51

Davis Dam 15
Denison Dam 73
Desolation Canyon 10
Diaz, Melchior 114
Dirty Devil River 10
disease 26, 36, 72
Dominguez, Francisco Atanasio 104
donkeys 12
drought 4, 113
dumping 60
Dust Bowl 35, 37, 38
dust storms 35–36, 37

1889 Land Run *27*
economy vii, 37
El Camino Real de Tierra Adentro *103*
electricity 14, 15, 73
environment 16, 124, 126
Escalante, Silvestre Vélez de 104
Europeans vii, viii, 5, 22, 46, 64, 102,
  103, 114

exodusters 35
exploration vii, viii, x, 7, 21, 22, 24, 44,
    46, 47, 48, 63, 64, 67, 82, 102, 114, 118

farming viii, ix, 14, 15, 34, 35, 37, 38, 39,
    41, 63, 94, 117, 121
    citrus 53, 94
    cotton 34, 39, 53, 94, 113, 120
    fruits 120
    hay 39
    peanuts 39
    rice 53
    vegetables 53, 94, 113, 120
    wheat 34, 39, 75, 120
Federal Aviation Administration (FAA) 16
fishing 11, 15, 45, 53, 54
    flounder 54
    shellfish 45
    shrimp 54
flooding 14, 15, 76, 121
Florida 46, 82
Fort St. Louis 48
Fra Cristobal Mountains 106
Frémont, John C. 106
French 48, 62, 65, 85

Gadsden Purchase 91, 118
Gadsden, James 118
Geographical and Geological Survey of
    the Rocky Mountain Region 8
Georgia 26
gila monster 123
Gila River 2, 113, 117, 119, 121, 122
Gila Trail 118
Glen Canyon Dam 11, 15
Glenn Pool 39
gold rush—see mining, gold
Goodnight, Charles 30
Goodnight-Loving Trail 33
Grand Canyon 3, 5, 6, 7, 9–10, 11,
    12, 16, 18
Grand Canyon game Reserve 18
Grand Canyon National Park 4, 17
Grand Canyon Trust, The 18
Grapes of Wrath, The 38
"Great American Desert" 24
Great Basin 8
Great Depression, The 37
Great Plains 20–25, 29, 31, 34–35, 39–42,
    64, 101
Green River 7
gulf coast 44, 45, 49, 51, 53–55, 57
Gulf Intracoastal Waterway 55
Gulf of California 2, 114
Gulf of Mexico vii, 44–47, 52, 59, 80, 84

Harquahala Mountains 113
Hoover Dam 13, 15

horses 23, 24, 25, 41, 64
hotels 12
Houston Ship Channel 55
Houston, Sam 50, 86
Hudson Bay 45
hunting viii, 3, 64
    buffalo 22, 23, 24, 29, 68, 70, 101
    deer 45
    mammoths 22
hurricanes 51, 52, 53, 57

Illinois
    Chicago 32
immigration
    Mexican 93
Imperial Canal 15
Imperial Dam 15
Imperial National Wildlife Refuge 123
Imperial Valley 15
Indian Removal Act 25, 70
International Balloon Festival 96, 97
ironwood 113
irrigation 39, 81, 94, 114, 120
Italian 117
Ives, Lieutenant Joseph 7, 10

Jackson, President Andrew 70
Japan 53
Jefferson, President Thomas 66, 67
jojoba 120
Joshua tree 113, 123
Joshua Tree National Park 123

Kansas 25, 35, 36, 38, 64, 83
    Abilene 32
    Atchinson 109
    Dodge City 32, 33
Kansas-Nebraska Act 26
Kearny, Stephan Watts 104, 105
Kinney, Henry Lawrence 49
Kino, Eusebio Francisco 114, 117
Kofa Mountains 113
Kofa National Wildlife Refuge 123

La Salle, René-Robert Cavelier, sieur de
    48, 64, 65, 84–85
Labyrinth Canyon 10
Lafitte, Jean 48, 49
Lake Mead 15
Lake Powell 15
Lake Texoma 73
land runs 27
Lincoln, President Abraham 69, 90
Little Colorado River 2
Llano Estacado 21
Long, Stephen 24
Louisiana 54, 62, 65, 67, 75, 77, 85
    New Orleans 34, 49, 54, 75

Louisiana Purchase 24, 66
Lyndon B. Johnson Space Center *58*, 59

manufacturing 94, 96, 122
Marcy, Randolph B. 67
Matagorda Bay 48, 84
Mather Point *17*
McClellan, George 67, *69*
Mexican Americans 91
Mexican Revolution 92
Mexican War viii, 7, 49, 88–91, 104, 118
Mexicans vii
Mexico vii, viii, 5, 6, 7, 23, 46, 48, 51, 68,
  80, 81, 82, 85, 86, 87, 88, 89, 91, 93, 96,
  98, 102, 104, 112, 113, 118, 123
  Chihuahua 85
  Matamoros 88
  Mexico City 89, 103
migration 37
military bases 122
mining
  coal 94
  copper 11, 122
  gold 10, 11, 68, 118, 122, 123
  gypsum 94
  lead 11, 122
  potash 94
  silver 11, 94, 122
missions 23, 83–84, 85, 103, 104, 114
Mississippi River 48, 59, 62, 66
Missouri
  Independence 107
  Kansas City 33
Montana 32

National Aeronautics and Space
  Administration (NASA) *58*, 59
National Parks Conservation
  Association 18
Native Americans vii, viii, ix, 5, 9, 21,
  25, 26, 32, 64, 67, 70, 75, 96, 101, 109,
  117, 119
  Anasazi viii, 4–5, 12
  Apache 23–24, 64, 68
  Arapaho 71, 72
  Arikara 63
  Atakapa 45
  Caddo viii, 63, 64
  Chemehuevi 5
  Cherokee 25, 26, 71
  Cheyenne 29, 64, 71, 72
  Chickasaw 25, 71
  Choctaw 25, 71
  Clovis viii, 22
  Coahuiltec 45, 81
  Comanche viii, 23–24, 25–26, 29, 64,
    68, 70, 72
  Cotoname 81

Creek 25, 71
Folsom viii, 22, 101
Havasupai 5
Hohokam 113, 120
Hopi 5
Jumano 81
Karankawa 45, 48
Kiowa viii, 23, 29, 64, 68, 70, 72
Mohave 5
Nasoni 63
Navajo 5
Osage 64
Paiute 5
Papago 119
Pawnee 63
Pima 113, 114
Plainview 22
Pueblo viii, 4, 81, 83–84, 101, 103
Seminole 71
Tampachoa 81
Tohono O'odham viii, 114, 119
Ute 5, 9
Wichita 64, 67
Yaqui 114
Ysleta *84*
Yuma viii, 114, 117, 119
Zuñi 5
natural gas ix, 45, 55, 57, 94
natural resources vii, 21, 40, 45, 53, 57,
  67, 101
Nebraska 25
Nevada viii, 2, 3, 15, 38, 89
New Jersey 69
New Mexico vii, x, 21, 23, 30, 36, 38, 80,
  83, 89, 91, 94, 100, 101, 106, 107, 118
  Albuquerque 83, 96, 97, 103
  Belen 103
  Carlsbad 22, 101
  Cerro 82
  Curry County 62
  Hot Springs 98
  Los Alamos *109*
  Santa Fe *ix*, 83, 85
  Taos 81, 101, 106, 110
New Spain—*see* Mexico
North America 100, 112
North American continent 100
North Pole 20, 68
North Sea 45
Nueces River 88

Ocampo, Sebastián de 46
Ogallala Aquifer 40
oil ix, 39, 45, 55, 57, 93
Oklahoma vii, ix, x, 21, 23, 24, 25, 26, 29,
  33, 35, 36, 38, 40, 41, 63, 64, 67, 70,
  72–73, 75, 76, 77
  Chelsea 39

Guymon *36*
Okeene *75*
Oklahoma City 40
Tulsa *39*, 40
Old Spanish Trail 104
Oñate, Juan de 83, 102, 114
100th meridian 68
Organ Pipe Cactus Monument *115*, 123

Pacific Ocean 5
Padre Island 51
Padre Island National Seashore 58
Parker Dam 15
Parker, Chief Quanah *28*, 29, 72
Parker, Cynthia 25, *28*
Pecos River 22, 81, 101
Pike, Zebulon 85
Piñeda, Alonso Álvarez de 46
pioneers 21
Polk, President James K. 88, 89, 90
pollution 16, 41, 59, 98, 124
Popé 83
population viii, 3, 26, 37, 40, 59, 77, 81,
    118, 119, 124
port cities 46, 54, 55, 57
Powell, John Wesley 7, *8*, 9, 10, 12
Prairie Dog Town Fork 64, 67
preservation 16
Pueblo Bonito 4
Pueblo Revolt of 1680 83–84
Pueblo Ysleta *84*

rafts 9, 75
railroad 10, 32, 34
rainfall 21, 35, 40, 120
ranching ix, 30, 34, 76, 94, 117, 120
rapids 7, 12
Red River 24, 62–65, 67–68, 70, 72–73,
    75–78, 81
Red River Compact Commission (RCC)
    77
Red River Station 76, 77
Red River War 72
refrigeration 34
Rio Grande River 59, 68, 80–83, 85–86,
    88–89, 92–94, 96, 98
Rio Grande Valley 81
Rio Grande/Rio Bravo Basin Coalition 98
Rivera, Juan de 103
Rocky Mountains 2, 20, 66, 80, 100–104,
    106, 109
Roosevelt Dam *121*, 122
Roosevelt, President Theodore 18,
    28, 122
Route 66 37

Saguaro 112, 123
salt 15, 64, 78

Salt River 113, 119, 121, 122
Salton Sea 15
San Jacinto Monument, The *87*
San Juan Mountains 80, 100, 102
San Juan Pueblo 83
Sangre de Cristo Mountains 100, 101,
    102, 107
Santa Anna, Antonia López de 86, *87*, 88
Santa Fe Railroad 12
Santa Fe River 81
Santa Fe Trail *106*, 107, 109
Scott, General Winfield 89
seasons vii, 14, 44, 112, 123
secession 50
settlement 3, 10, 25, 26, 42, 44, 47, 51,
    68, 75, 83–84, 85, 101, 117, 119
Shawnee Trail 33, 68
shipping 10, 32, 54
shipwrecks 51, 82
Shreve, Captain Henry Miller 75, 76
Sibley, Dr. John 67
slaughterhouses 34
Smithsonian Institute's
    Bureau of Ethnology *8*
Sonoran Desert 112–114, *115*, 117,
    120–124, 126
"Sooners" *27*
South Pole 20, 68
Southern Pacific Railroad 119
Southwestern International Livestock
    Show and Rodeo *32*
Spain 46, 68, 83, 85, 103, 114
Spanish vii, viii, ix, 5, 7, 21, 30, 46, 48,
    51, 62, 63, 64, 65, 67, 68, 81, 82, 83–84,
    85, 86, 94, *95*, 96, 103, 109, 113, 114
sports teams 124
steamboats 7, *77*
Steinbeck, John 38
Straits of Florida 44
Swilling, Jack 120

Taliesin West *125*
Taylor, General Zachary 49, 88, 89
Texas vii, x, 7, 20, 21, 23, 29, 30, 32, 34,
    36, 38, 40, 44, 47, 48, 50, 54, 57, 60, 62,
    63, 64, 67, 68, 72–73, 75, 77, 80, 82, 85,
    88, 91, 92, 94, 98, 101
    Austin 33
    Bandera 33
    Beaumont 54, 55
    Brazos 46
    Brownsville 44, 55, 80, 88, 91, 94, 98
    Colbert's Ferry 68
    Corpus Christi 45, 46, 49, 53, 54, 55,
        57, 58
    Dallas viii
    Del Rio *96*
    Doan's Crossing 68

El Paso 83, *84*, 98
Fort Myers 55
Fort Parker 25
Freeport 54
Galveston 45, 46, 48, 51, 53, *54*
Gonzales 86
Houston viii, 51, 53, 54, 57, 59
Matagorda 46
Montague County 76
Mustang 46
Padre Island 46
Pecos *22*
Port Isabel 54
Rio Grande City 98
Rock Bluff 68
Sabine 44
San Antonio viii, 33, 88
Spindletop 55, *56*, 57
Texas City 52, 54
Vernon 62, 77
Young County 33
Texas longhorn cattle 33
Texas Rangers 92
Texas Revolution 86, 88
textiles 94
topsoil 38
tornadoes 29–30, *31*
tourism 11, 12, 16–17, 58, 96,
    109–110, 123
trading 11, 65, 75–76, 80, 104, 106,
    109, 118
trading posts 49, 75
trapping 11, 65, 109, 118
Treaty of Guadalupe Hildalgo 7, 89, 118
tributaries 2, 7, 81
Tusayan Pueblo 5
Tyler, President John 88

United States vii, viii, ix, 7, 20, 24, 29, 37,
    62, 63, 66, 67, 68, 72, 80, 81, 86, 88, 89,
    91, 92, 93, 96, 102, 104, 118
    Midwest vii, 21, 40, 107, 109
    New England 36
    North 30, *76*
    Northeast 40, 94
    Southeast vii, 40, 71
    West vii, 13, 15, 21, 30, 85, 100, 104
United States
    Geological Survey (USGS) *8*
U.S. Army 25, 29, *67*, 85
U.S. government 25, 26, 27, 29, 38, 41,
    68, 72, 122
U.S. Postal Service *103*
U.S. Supreme Court 72, 73, 122
U.S. troops 26, *49*, 91, 122
Utah 2, 89, 104

War of 1812 *49*
Washington, D.C. 36
water supply 3, 35, 40, 41, 78, 98,
    120, 122
waterfalls 7
Western Trail 33, 77
Whirlpools 9
White, James 9
Wilson, President Woodrow 17
World War II 54, 122
Wright, Frank Lloyd *125*
Wyoming 7, 89

Yucatán Channel 44